Mindfulness and Relaxation Activities for All Ages

AF736701

This practical guide to mindfulness activities provides ready-to-use scripts that readers can use to deliver calming, soothing and grounding activities to young people of all ages, including adults.

This book showcases evidence-based scripts for activities to develop relaxation, mindfulness, self-compassion, self-awareness and resilience in people of all ages. It aims to prompt the creative development of support activities that bring forward positive well-being responses. It provides over 60 ready-to-present activity scripts and includes visualisations, movement and stillness games and meditations and recommendations for creative expression to integrate and understand the experiences. The chapters indicate the age range for whom the activities are designed. Chapter 2 provides activities that prepare participants for engagement in the activities. Chapters 3 and 4 focus on activities for younger people, Chapter 5 is designed for young adolescents and the activities in Chapter 6 are designed for presenting to older adolescents, as well as adults. Through this book, readers will be able to apply age-appropriate activities that can lead participants of all ages to improved clarity, focus, calmness and an enhanced positive sense of self.

Written by a leading professional with four decades' experience in clinical counselling, university teaching and creative arts therapies, this is an essential child- and adolescent-friendly resource that includes activities for adults to participate in, and can be used by counsellors, psychologists, mental health professionals, educators, parents and all those who provide well-being care for people of all ages.

Mark Pearson, PhD, has been conducting courses in Expressive Therapies for over 36 years, was a counsellor for clients of all ages for 28 years and lectured in counselling at four Australian universities for 20 years. He holds a PhD, a Master's in Education – Behaviour Management – and a Diploma of Teaching.

Mindfulness and Relaxation Activities for All Ages

Over Sixty Fun and Engaging Evidence-based Visualisations, Meditations and Self-awareness Games

Mark Pearson

Routledge
Taylor & Francis Group
LONDON AND NEW YORK

Designed cover image: Getty images

First published 2026
by Routledge
4 Park Square, Milton Park, Abingdon, Oxon OX14 4RN

and by Routledge
605 Third Avenue, New York, NY 10158

Routledge is an imprint of the Taylor & Francis Group, an informa business

British Library Cataloguing-in-Publication Data
A catalogue record for this book is available from the British Library

ISBN: 9781041204398 (hbk)
ISBN: 9781041204381 (pbk)
ISBN: 9781003716501 (ebk)

DOI: 10.4324/9781003716501

Typeset in Galliard
by codeMantra

For use by counsellors, psychologists, teachers, chaplains and behaviour specialists, in groupwork and individually.

Contents

By the Same Author xi
Acknowledgements xiii
About the Author xv
Preface xvii

1 Introduction and Evidence Base 1
About This Book 1
Introduction to the Activities 2
Preparation and Background to the Activities 4
Therapeutic Presence for Presenters 4
Rapport Building 5
Why Is Rapport Important? 6
Materials Needed 6
Use of Music during and after Activities 7
Delivery of the Activities 7
Helping Participants Breathe Fully 8
Difficulties with Quiet Inner Focus 8
Use of Movement 9
Written Reflection after Activities 9
Artistic Expression after Activities 10
A Note on Group Work 12
A Language for the Inner World 15
Guided Mental Imagery and Visualisation 16
Reducing Participants' Self-criticism 18
Using Positive Memory and Mental Imagery 18
A Discussion on Relaxation 19
A Discussion on Mindfulness 20
Contraindications for Using Mindfulness 22
Offering Advice on Developing a Mindfulness Practice 23
Creative Expression after Mindfulness Practice 24
A Discussion on Self-compassion 26

2 Preparation and Rapport-Building Activities: Creating Safety; Supporting Freedom with Art and Writing 28

Safety Visualisation: My Safe and Beautiful Place in Nature *29*

Using Breath to Support Opening Up: Ways to Take Deep Breaths *30*

Exploring Self-talk Habits: Discussing Criticism and Self-kindness *31*

Self-reflection Writing: How Self-compassionate Are You? *32*

Mandala Freedom: Colouring Circles with the Wrong Hand *34*

Mandala Freedom: Drawing Music *35*

Speed Art: Drawing Feelings *36*

Written Reflections: Sentence Starters *37*

Reflection with Clay: My Feelings in Clay *38*

Getting to Know You Discussion: Who Are We? *39*

Somatic Awareness Practice: What's Happening in My Body? *40*

Reflecting on Relaxation: What Helps You Relax and Play? *41*

3 A Fern in the Forest: Visualisation, Relaxation and Stillness Stories for Young People 7–10 Years 42

Relaxation Story: A Fern in the Forest *43*

Breathing Games: Balloons and Whales *45*

Visualisation Story: An Iceberg Melts *47*

Active Relaxation: Moving in Slow Motion *49*

The Lazy Relaxation: You Don't Have to Do Anything *50*

Visualising Beauty: My Favourite Place in Nature *52*

Visualising Peace: The Peaceful Park *54*

Visualisation for Sleep: The Full Moon *55*

Visualisation for Rest: The Mountain Stream *56*

4 Imaginary Journeys: Visualisation, Role-Play and Movement Adventures for Relaxation and Resilience for Young People 7–10 Years 57

De-stressing and Energising: A Star in the Midnight Sky *58*

Visualising Peace: You Are the Sunset *60*

Movement Role-Play Game: A Seal on a Warm Rock *61*

Movement Role-Play Game: A Twister Unwinds *63*

Movement Role-Play Game: The Exploding Volcano *64*

Movement Role-Play Game: A Playful Cheetah in the Long Grass *65*

Movement Role-Play Game: A Colourful Snake beside the Creek *66*
Strength Visualisation: The Mysterious Island *67*
Strength Visualisation: The Shopping Trip – A Gift for You *69*
Role-Play of the Gift *70*
Time in Nature Visualisation: Ascent of the Mountain *71*
Wisdom Visualisation: The Wisest Person on Earth *73*

5 Sitting Still – Doing Nothing: Mindfulness, Meditation and Self-awareness for Young People 9–14 Years 75
Relaxation with Autogenic Phrases: Inviting Softness *76*
Relaxation through Vibration: The Humming Tunnel *77*
Guided Imagery for Self-esteem: Your Power Animal *80*
Movement Meditation: Bare Feet, Slow Walking *82*
Movement Meditation: Slower Than a Snail *84*
Grounding Visualisation: Finding Strength *86*
Review and Reflect: Not Yesterday, Not Tomorrow, Just Now *87*
Mental Imagery for Somatic Experience: My Four-Storey Building *89*
Somatic Focused Meditation: An Apple in My Hand *91*
Mindfulness Breath Meditation: The Air Flows In and Out *93*
Mindfulness Practice: The Sounds around Me *95*
Gratitude Reflections: My Gratitude Memories *96*
Sitting Meditation: In My Bubble – Sitting Still, Doing Nothing *97*

6 Tuning In, Taking Time, Caring for Self: Mindfulness, Reflection and Self-compassion for Adolescents and Adults 99
Introducing Mindfulness: Some Necessary Attitudes *99*
Somatic Focus Grounding: Body Scan *101*
Somatic Focus Grounding: Listening Inside *103*
Self-kindness Practice: May I Learn to Accept Myself *104*
Progressive Relaxation: Tension and Surrender *105*
Mindfulness Practice: Here and Now – In This Moment *107*
Grounding and Centring: A Window to My Inner World *109*
Mindful Movement: Slow-Motion for Self-awareness *110*
Visualisation and Role-Play: I Am Nature *111*
Sitting Practice: What Can I Hear Around Me? *112*
Visualisation for Personal Growth: No Stone Unturned *113*
Mindful Energy Focus: Finding My Neutral Observer *114*

Visualisation: A Glimpse of My Potential *115*
Relaxation and Guided Meditation: Can I Find a Quiet Centre? *116*
Expressing Reflections: Finding Myself in Nature *117*
Energy Centre Meditation: Heart and Belly Focus *118*

Appendix: Suggested Background Music for Relaxation, Meditation Background *119*
References *120*
Index *125*

By the Same Author

Pearson, M., & Wilson, H. (2001). *Sandplay and symbol work. Emotional healing and personal development with children, adolescents and adults.* ACER Press.

Pearson, M. (2004). *Emotional healing and self-esteem: Inner-life skills of relaxation, visualisation and meditation for children and adolescents.* Jessica Kingsley Publishers.

Pearson, M., & Nolan, P. (2004). *Emotional release for children: Repairing the past, preparing the future.* Jessica Kingsley Publishers.

Pearson, M., & Wilson, H. (2009). *Using expressive arts to work with mind, body and emotions. Theory and practice.* Jessica Kingsley Publishers.

Pearson, M., & Wilson, H. (2026). *Counselling children and adolescents with expressive therapies. Creative arts activities to inspire wellbeing.* Routledge.

Find the author's peer-reviewed academic articles at: https://expressivetherapies.au/publications.php

Acknowledgements

This collection would not exist without the input, challenges and encouragement of my partner in life and work, Dr Helen Wilson. I am blessed to have such partnership. Many of the ideas expressed in the activities offered here, and the overall Expressive Therapies theory and methods, emerged from our shared authorship of books and articles, our clinical practice and her valuable insights generated through extensive provision of clinical supervision for so many years.

I am also grateful for the inspiration from the writings of mindfulness pioneers, the creators of the Oxford Mindfulness-based Cognitive Therapy Program, on whose work some of these activities are based. Kristin Neff's research, exposition and teaching on self-compassion have also been a great foundation.

And I am also so grateful for the counselling clients who explored the early forms of these activities, the participants in our training courses who shared the activities with their own clients and those who provided valuable feedback.

About the Author

Mark Pearson began his career as a primary school teacher, working with children from 7 to 12 years, and then founded a remedial reading clinic, for which he began writing stories specially for different reading levels. Early in his career, he received several government creative writing scholarships and has continued his interest in writing. While remaining a novice in mindfulness practice – despite many years practice – as a counsellor and an educator, he enjoys finding ways of inspiring clients and students of all ages to move towards greater self-awareness and a stronger sense of self.

For over 28 years, he has worked as a counsellor, specialising in supporting young clients through creative arts-based approaches. Mark is the Co-director of *Expressive Therapies Australia* and has been conducting training courses in Expressive Therapies and Sandplay Therapy around Australia since 1989, and in Southeast Asia since 2001. As well as counselling studies, he has completed training in Transpersonal Psychotherapy and holds a Master's in Education, majoring in behaviour management and a PhD researching the use of multiple intelligences in counselling.

Mark lectured in counselling at four Australian universities, teaching post-graduate counselling students. He specialised in teaching the practice and professional application of mindfulness in counselling practices, as well as delivering expressive therapies.

Mark is the author of *Emotional First-Aid for Children* (1991), *From Healing to Awakening* (1991), *The Healing Journey* (1997), *Emotional Healing & Self-Esteem – Inner-Life Skills for Children and Adolescents* (2004), *Emotional Release for Children* (2004) and *The Expressive Therapies Groupwork Program: Innerspace* (2006). He is the co-author, with Helen Wilson, of *Sandplay & Symbol Work* (2001), *Using Expressive Arts to Work with Mind, Body and Emotion* (2009) and *Child and Adolescent Counselling with Expressive Therapies: Creative Arts Activities to Inspire Wellbeing* (2026).

Many of Mark's peer-reviewed articles are available at: https://expressivetherapies.au/publications.php

Feedback on the activities in this book is welcomed at: mark@expressivetherapies.au

Preface

This book provides over 60 tried and true, evidence-based scripts for activities to develop relaxation, mindfulness, self-compassion, self-awareness and resilience in people of all ages. The ready-to-use scripts are a valuable resource for counsellors, psychologists, mental health professionals, educators and all those who provide well-being care for young people. It is highly suitable for parents to use at home with the family.

The activities are designed to help people of all ages enjoy increasing self-awareness and reduce stress and anxiety. It also has an aim of inspiring the reader's application and creative development of support activities that bring forward positive well-being responses.

The evidence base grows for the benefits and these approaches are used more routinely in counselling, psychotherapy, in schools and in community centres. There particularly has been growing interest from schools to include these types of activities in well-being classroom programmes. Child-friendly adaptations of traditional mindfulness activities can prove valuable for building attentional skills. Increases in the ability to focus attention can contribute to a wide range of academic learning tasks, life skills and social cohesion.

Why is it a good idea to practice relaxation? In the world today, there is so much that makes us tense, stressed and worried. Each day we spend so much time looking at, and listening to, everything around us. We can so easily get used to worrying. Relaxation activities give us time to let go, become quiet and still for a moment and feel happier. Scientists tell us that these types of relaxation and mindfulness activities are good for our health, good for our brains and can increase well-being. Our bodies work better when we are relaxed. Our mind is clearer and more positive when we are not lost in concerns about the past and the future.

There are many types of mindfulness and relaxation activities in this book; some use movement, some use imagination, some help us to be still and quiet and some can help us get to sleep at night. Relaxation can help us feel warm and soft, concentrate better on the work we need to do and enjoy play and rest. Mindfulness can help us enjoy moments of pleasure and fun, as well as reduce overwhelm in stressful times.

Through being a provider of training in counselling and the creative arts therapies for over 36 years, I have had many counsellors, school psychologists, guidance officers, teachers and well-being staff ask about ways to introduce some of the mindfulness methods for both young people and adults. They seek easy-to-use, creative ways to extend students' and clients' ability to focus and pay attention, to be grounded and to be more self-aware.

This book has grown out of extensive collaborations with my partner and colleague, Dr Helen Wilson, and through trialling some activities in my private practice as a counsellor. The formulation of the activities for young people has been informed by my first career as a primary school teacher. Many of the activities for adolescents and adults have been inspired by the mindfulness research of Kabat-Zin and the self-compassion research of Neff. The activities have been trialled by me, by Helen and by our students who have provided formal feedback within supervision. The activities have been developed over the last ten years to support my role as a therapy and well-being tertiary educator and personal development presenter.

The ready-to-present activity scripts include visualisations, movement and stillness games and meditations, and recommendations for creative expression to integrate and understand the experiences. The chapters indicate the age range for whom the activities are designed. Chapters 3 and 4 focus on activities for younger people, Chapter 5 is designed for young adolescents, and Chapter 6 presents activities designed for older adolescents as well as adults.

1 Introduction and Evidence Base

About This Book

This book is a practical resource for counsellors, psychotherapists, psychologists, educators, behaviour specialists and all those who provide well-being care for others. It provides tried and true, evidence-based scripts for activities to develop mindfulness, relaxation, self-compassion, self-awareness and resilience in clients and students of all ages. This book has an aim of inspiring your application and creative development of support activities that bring forth positive well-being responses. From over 36 years of experience as a counsellor and educator specialising in creative arts therapies, I am pleased to share the scripts for my best practical mindfulness and relaxation activities.

The next section of this chapter shares some of the evidence base that underpins the activities. Within the discussions on mindfulness and self-compassion, you will find some of the research on these practices and other components of the activities, including information about outcomes and capacities developed through these practices.

The activities have been developed for use by counsellors, therapists, psychologists, social workers, teachers, behaviour specialists and parents who wish to advance the well-being of the people they care for. The activities are suitable for individual or group practice and have also been found to enhance relaxation at bedtime, supporting better sleep.

This book provides ready-to-present activity scripts and includes visualisations, movement and stillness games and meditations, invitations to self-reflection, as well as recommendations for creative expression to integrate experience arising from the activities. The chapters indicate the age range for whom the activities are designed. You will see that Chapter 2 covers

DOI: 10.4324/9781003716501-1

introductory activities that prepare participants for engagement. Chapters 3 and 4 focus on activities for younger people, Chapter 5 is designed for young adolescents, and Chapter 6 presents activities designed for older adolescents and adults.

Chapter 1 sets the scene and provides some background to the activities in this book. It provides some guidelines for presenters and gives a brief background to mindfulness, relaxation and self-compassion.

Chapter 2 provides introductory activities that prepare participants for engagement in the activities. Some activities here are designed to support rapport development, create a sense of safety, and provide short orientations to the practices in the activities. A few activities in Chapter 2 are recommended to familiarise participants with ways of integrating their experiences from the activity sessions, through creative expression. Some activities are designed for building connections when working with groups.

Chapter 3 provides child-friendly mindfulness and relaxation activities, and is designed for supporting young people from approximately 7 to 10 years. The activities, games and stories blend skills in visualisation, use of breath, relaxation and focusing attention in order to support relaxation and well-being. There are recommendations for the integration of activities through artistic expression.

Chapter 4 is also designed for supporting young people from approximately 7 to 10 years. The activities, games and stories blend skills in somatic awareness, controlled movement, relaxation, visualisation, emotional expression, playfulness and focused attention in order to support ability with relaxation, enhanced self-esteem and resilience.

Chapter 5 is designed to support young people from approximately 9 to 14 years. The activities and meditations blend skills in self-awareness, conscious movement and focus on breath and body, as doorways to developing a mindful state.

Chapter 6 is designed to support older adolescents and adults. The meditative activities develop skills in self-awareness, reflection, self-compassion and mindful focus, as doorways to deepening relaxation, presence and well-being.

Introduction to the Activities

This book is full of mindfulness, relaxation, visualisation and self-compassion stories and activities, designed to help people of all ages enjoy turning their focus within, increasing self-awareness, and reducing stress and anxiety. Once participants in the activities gain experience in this style of self-exploration, motivation to explore further is enhanced. We have found that participation can lead to many requests to experience further activities, as well as return to some favourites.

We recommend the use of only one activity at a time. After each activity, we encourage participants to linger in a quiet, focused state and enjoy quiet creative time to draw or write about their experience of the activity.

There are many types of relaxation and mindfulness activities: some use movement, some use imagination, some help us to be still and quiet, and some can help us get to sleep at night. Relaxation helps us de-stress. Relaxation can help us feel warm and soft, concentrate better on the work we need to do, and enjoy play and rest. Mindfulness and self-compassion can help us move out of the past or future, and enjoy self-kindness in the moment.

Why is it a good idea to practice relaxation and mindfulness? In the world today, there is so much that makes us tense, stressed and worried. Each day we spend so much time looking at, and listening to, being drawn out by everything around us. Sometimes we worry about what others think about us, what might happen next, and what happened yesterday. We can get used to worrying. Relaxation and mindfulness activities give us time to let go of worries, become quiet and still for a moment, and feel more at home in ourselves.

What is the difference between relaxation and mindfulness? When we practice mindfulness, the aim is to become aware of what is happening inside, without trying to change anything. When practicing mindfulness, the aim is to keep coming back to self-focus; that is focus on our body, our mood, and our thoughts. The act of staying present in itself can be a catalyst for change. Additionally, we try to let go of any judgement about what we observe internally and return to an effort to extend our self-awareness. These practices are supported through efforts with self-compassion, as a way to step away from habits of self-criticism.

When we practice relaxation, we aim for a similar internal focus; however, we also actively give our body permission to let go of the everyday tensions that inevitably build up. Some people find they are more able to maintain an internal focus when they are already relaxed and calm. Relaxation activities often have some similarities with mindfulness practice, but also include various somatic, cognitive and metaphorical methods for connecting with tensions and allowing them to slide away.

Scientists tell us that these types of self-care activities are good for our health, good for our brains and can support happiness. Our bodies work better when we are relaxed and we are self-aware. Our mind is clearer and more positive when we are present and relaxed. We enjoy being with our friends more when we are focused and relaxed. These types of activities can help us feel calmer, think more clearly and have better connections with other people.

And, many of the world's great discoveries were made while people were relaxing, playing or resting! The research on creativity actually recommends allowing mind-wandering, daydreaming and play, so that creative thinking can spontaneously emerge. So, we might even find we are more creative and confident when we can connect more fully with ourselves and relax!

Some people may think mindfulness and relaxation practices are weird, and that sitting still or lying down quietly is boring, or perhaps impossible. But getting to know what is happening inside us can be very entertaining, as long as we don't get hooked into judging what we are trying to do! And seeing how long we can focus on the activity can be a challenge. Experience has shown that with practice, it becomes more and more possible to stay focused within these activities, even though we do have "good" days and "bad" days. Learning to tune in and relax will be very helpful throughout life, although it can be frustrating at first. With practice we are more able to let go of worries, stresses and upsets. Self-awareness and relaxation can help us find confidence and a feeling of strength.

When we tested out the activities in Chapters 2–5, some young people found that simply listening to the relaxation stories could help them get to sleep at night more easily, after a busy day.

Starting to tune in to what's happening inside us and relax may seem difficult. Many people notice they find it hard to concentrate on the activities at first, they keep thinking of other things, and some notice that they are agitated, tense or restless. This is quite normal. So, if you notice during an activity you are not paying attention, or you are thinking about yesterday or tomorrow, or wondering what people outside are saying or doing, all you have to do is take a deep breath, focus inside yourself and start to pay attention to the activity again. It does not matter how often you have to start over!

For the activities in this book, we recommend you try them sitting in a comfortable chair, or while lying on a soft carpet, with a pillow under your head. In general, sitting up for mindfulness and reflection; lying down for relaxation. The activities are useful in group work, as well as used individually.

After each activity, we recommend participants try some creative expression, maybe some drawing or writing. This is a way to reflect on the activity and your experiences of yourself. Even if people are not used to drawing or think that they are not so good at it, they could create something with abstract colours, shapes and lines and maybe add some words to it. This would be an individual way to keep a record of moods, feelings and thoughts after the activity.

I hope you enjoy using these activities. My wish for you is that you try the activities many times and learn to find more calm, clear and relaxed enjoyment of your life.

Preparation and Background to the Activities

Therapeutic Presence for Presenters

How we are – our inner state – while in our role as a presenter can be just as important, in terms of participant responsiveness and engagement, as what we offer. Our own mindfulness practice can support the development of therapeutic presence. When we empty out, we permit a creative space within, which allows space for the other's experience (Hycner & Jacobs, 1995). Presence means to set aside our own needs, vulnerability and injuredness, and to be able to open to the injured and disowned parts of another. "If I am too full of myself there is no room for the other" (Hycner & Jacobs, 1995, p. 49).

Therapeutic presence is the state of having one's whole self in the encounter with another by being completely in the moment on a multiplicity of levels – physically, emotionally, cognitively and spiritually. This grounded, immersed and expanded awareness occurs with the intention of being with and for the other, in service to his or her healing process (Geller & Greenberg, 2012).

A Way of Being for Presenters

These are some recommended relational aims for those presenting the activities in this book:

- Operate from a field of openness and curiosity about how the participant(s) may respond
- Activate participants' interest in self-discovery and self-exploration
- Validate any feelings they report
- Try to meet them "where they are"
- Help them develop trust with you, with self and with others if in a group
- Model and reinforce acceptance and rapport

Aim to use an invitational style of relating:

- Invite rather than instruct
- Invitations encourage reflection and commitment to participate
- Invitations to participate create an atmosphere of respect, which allows greater student involvement
- Model respect
- Allow choice where possible
- Offer a question rather than a statement
- Draw out observations from participants, rather than making them
- Evoke "allowing" rather than "doing", i.e.,
  - *See what comes to mind rather than think of this.*
- Examples of invitational relating might include:
  - *Would you like to …*
    - *say something more about that?*
    - *tell me what happened?*
  - *Do you feel ready to… move on to the next activity?… share how that felt?*

Rapport Building

Building rapport is central to supporting engagement. Rapport is needed between participant and presenter, and among participants in group work.

Early in the presenter–participant relationship, the aim is to develop trust. Early in the development of group relationships, there needs to be non-challenging ways to build connection (see activity "Getting to Know You" on page 39).

Recommendations for Early Sessions

- Make time for participants to develop trust – in you, the setting, and the activities you will offer. This can be supported by providing brief reasons for the group and for each activity.
- Address their perception of why they think they have come, or been sent, to be part of the group.
- Provide some options for engagement activities, e.g., eyes open or closed, being still or moving.
- Assist them to develop trust in themselves and create language with which they can articulate their preferences, experiences of the activities, as well as their needs and wants.
- Allow apprehension, resistance or anxiety about participation to come forward, and if needed, be discussed and addressed before moving on.
- Invite participants to introduce themselves, to talk about themselves and their lives.
- Provide an overview of the options for expression after the activities.

Why Is Rapport Important?

Research into what promotes positive therapy outcomes makes it clear that growth and change are related to what clients engage with in sessions, what theories underlie the methods we use, but are most strongly influenced by how we relate with clients as individuals, and our ability to engage them in the process. Good techniques are associated with a good alliance (Muran & Barber, 2010). Baylis et al. (2011) identified further behaviours on which alliance – according to their young clients – was dependent: being nice, active listening and expressions of caring.

Presenters and therapists need to pay particular attention to the relationship with participants or clients, and find ways to enhance what the participant contributes. As we provide here activity-based interventions, young participants are most likely to engage readily. They prefer to "do something" rather than talk about internal experiences. We like to emphasise the importance of taking time to develop connection, prior to offering the activities, or indeed any intervention.

Materials Needed

Some form of artistic expression after the activities can be valuable to consolidate and to make meaning of the experience, particularly of any challenges the activity evoked. It is recommended that you have some drawing paper and crayons, and a pen close by to support participants to reflect on their experience, draw and/or write something after each activity. This encourages them to stay within a quiet space and to gain simple skills in self-reflection, expressing, documenting and reinforcing their experience.

Use of Music during and after Activities

In the Appendix (see page 119), you will find some of our suggestions for useful background music. Music can contribute to creating a safe "holding space" that allows participants to feel safe and private. Always check – before starting – participants' responses to the music. Offering some quiet background music after the activities, while participants express their experiences, can be very helpful to support focus. And, of course, there may be times when silence is more suitable.

Using Music in the Background

- Take time to become familiar with the music equipment.
- When changing, starting or stopping a track, turn volume down and then up, so there are no shocks from sudden volume.
- Does the activity call for consistent rhythm? Or, no rhythm at all?
- Check the melody, is it in the foreground or background, is it too attractive or emotionally scripting?
- Are the volume and speed of the music consistent?
- Usually best to avoid vocals, or songs in a language the client can understand, as this can bring in extraneous cognitive activity.

Delivery of the Activities

Clear instructions contribute to a feeling of safety. When giving or reading instructions, look carefully at the participant or group. Ask yourself:

- Have they heard the instructions?
- Have the instructions been understood?
- Do you need to repeat or rephrase?
- And, of course, feel free to rephrase in a way that supports your flow.

Tips for Preparing for, and Reflecting on, Your Delivery

- Read through and try out the activities carefully before presentation.
- It is ideal that you experience the activity yourself before presenting it. So, ask a colleague to take you through the steps in the way you are going to present them.
- In group work: Invite the group to choose partners for debriefing before starting the activity.
- Frequently relax your own body, and take a few deep breaths before giving instructions.

- Is your voice carrying to the far side of the room?
- Do you need to slow down or speed up the delivery?
- Give directions at least twice.
- Give only one direction at a time.
- Modulate or regulate background music as the activity requires.
- Steadily reduce the volume of music prior to and when giving instructions.

Helping Participants Breathe Fully

Within the activities in this book, you will find frequent invitations to participants to take some deep breaths. From the discoveries of Grof's depth psychotherapeutic process (Grof, Grof & Kornfield, 2010) comes the extended use of breath to open up the psyche in a therapeutic process. Many approaches to physical and mental health use breath (Victoria & Caldwell, 2013). Most particularly, this is a function in body-oriented psychotherapy. The well-documented positive physical effects of good breathing can have "a profound influence on psychological well-being, particularly in the areas of mood, the reduction of negative emotion and an increase in positive emotion, emotional regulation and the capacity for social engagement" (Victoria & Caldwell, 2013, p. 217).

Reducing the speed and depth of breathing seems to be one way the body can defend against (usually unpleasant) internal experience. On page 30, you will find some breathing games that can support and empower a participant's ability with self-awareness. The background approach to counselling from which the activities in this book were developed – Expressive Therapies – incorporates multiple ways to engage young people in taking deeper breaths, to play with breath and to role-play creatures that display lots of breath, for example, fire-breathing dragons, whales and dogs panting after a long run on a winter morning.

Difficulties with Quiet Inner Focus

Agitation is a major difficulty in the practice of quiet inner focus, such as meditation and mindfulness. Agitation can have many causes. It can be the result of an emotional upset, a high level of physical energy – that does not want to be quiet and still – or some emotional stress that a person is unaware of. High levels of cortisol (Jones & Gwenin, 2021) can be released in response to stress or perceived threats, fuelling muscles for action. There will be times when a young person is dealing with distress, has higher levels of cortisol and cannot participate. It is natural that in the case of emotional disturbance or trauma recovery, attention will be constantly directed away from unpleasant internal experience.

The requirement, or the effort, to be still can highlight the emotional stress, even making it appear that the activity has caused it! Young people who carry a high level of turmoil will usually avoid or resent internal focus at first and react against it with distractions. Tension that is held in the body can come to awareness during stillness. Emotional or physical holding that has not been noticed in the busyness of life can be discovered during quiet times, and this is uncomfortable. A presenter may need to be prepared to allow for some stretching, shaking, and movement to release the physical holding before, during or even after the quiet inward-focused activities.

A difficulty to be avoided is setting up expectations. The aims or possible outcomes of the activities should always be provided in a general way so that no specific outcome is anticipated. Each of us is different, and we experience differently. We can often experience exactly the same activity quite differently at different times. This will depend on our mood, energy level, motivation, levels of emotional stress, interest, timing of the activity, as well as immediately prior activities, e.g., soccer practice. So, in an effort to meet participants "where they are", more physically engaging activities may need to precede quiet inner focus.

Connected with expectations is the unfortunate role of our inner critic, the self-judging part of the psyche. If we hold negative beliefs about ourselves – as most of us do to some extent, and many young people do – prescribed activity outcomes could be interpreted as proving negative beliefs about self. Support for young people to recognise, and then drop self-criticism, is essential. Presenters should never add to these self-doubts by highlighting their inability to focus, be still and quiet. Engagement in the activities should always be offered as a learning process, with steps, however small, being identified each time.

Use of Movement

Chapters 3 and 4, in particular, include movement within the activities. Several activities open with an invitation to stand, stretch, shake or run and take some deep breaths. These movements are intended to help a participant increase somatic connection and reduce tension, to ease their way into an activity. After somatic activation, it is often much more possible to make a connection with the body and internal processes.

Movement has been shown to increase cognitive ability and concentration (Peiris et al., 2021). If you notice a participant needing to move, improvise an opportunity to go with that impulse, e.g., wriggle, shake, run on the spot, and gather something from the other side of the room. This will support increased focus and engagement with the activity. Demands to remain strictly still (as are often included in meditation practices for adults) will be counterproductive. Make suggestions for exploring stillness as invitations, questions, experiments, not demands or commands.

Written Reflection after Activities

Self-reflective writing is a tool that can clarify thoughts, beliefs and emotions, and may support reflection on experiences during an activity and on participants' state after an activity. In a life where guided reflection and free expression may not have a safe space, writing about personal experiences can provide a source of quiet empowerment. Completion writing can also enhance integration after activities, through building both right and left hemisphere activation (Field, 2014).

The use of writing for therapeutic outcome has been linked to significant increases in personal well-being. Evidence from research over many decades shows a positive impact of expressive writing in many domains of physical and psychological health, particularly following trauma (Peterkin & Prettyman, 2009). Outcomes include enhanced immune functioning, improved liver enzyme function, reduced frequency of health centre visits and greater effectiveness in coping with job loss and regaining employment (Kenardy & Piercy, 2006; Pennebaker & Seagal, 1999). Additionally, the dawn of an expanded focus on the positive in Western psychology encouraged a turning of attention towards deepening experiences of satisfaction, gratitude, awe and well-being. Ruini and Mortara (2022) showed positive therapeutic effects on symptoms and distress, but also that writing can promote psychological well-being.

Completion writing is an integrative step (Pearson & Wilson, 2009); it brings cognitive focus, to summarise, to use left hemisphere functions to support closure after right hemisphere experience. For example, choosing three words to sum up an experience might be a good catalyst for reflection and communication. The activity of sentence completion can help integration, and it brings experiences together and makes meaning (see the activity on page 37).

Artistic Expression after Activities

Inviting a participant to express their internal experiences, after an activity, through the use of colours, lines, shapes, images, metaphors and words, provides a way for them to integrate and to make sense of their experience. It provides time and means for them to both reflect on and better communicate their experience, and it furthers their integration of internal experiences (McMurray & Schwartz–Mirman, 2001). For these reasons, we recommend inviting clients to follow the expression suggestions closing most of the activities. It can also be helpful to offer some quiet, calming background music that can act as a "holding space" after an activity, while expression is underway. This can signal to the individual that it is cool to remain quiet and focus on their art or writing. However, clients must also feel at ease if they prefer not to record or discuss their experiences.

It is vital that presenters do not offer interpretations of participants' artwork or any creative expression. Responses to art-making after an activity should be empowering for the participant, without suggesting meaning or offering too much praise about the final creation (as it is the process of expression that is helpful, not so much the end creation). It can be appropriate to invite a participant to share any feelings, thoughts, sensations or meaning that they see reflected in their art expression.

Why Use Circle Shapes for Artwork?

Creative expression with colours and lines in or around a circle – or mandala – has been found to be more calming than drawing on or in a rectangle or square (Kellogg, 1992).

Mandalas we create support integration or psychological and emotional experience. In a series – over time – they can form a valuable map that helps make sense of our exploration of internal experiences.

While in traditional cultures, such as Tibetan Buddhism, Navajo sand pictures and Australian Aboriginal sand art, mandalas can be complex and highly structured, mandala expression with young people is usually not premeditated; there is no requirement for them to be planned, but are "allowed" to flow out spontaneously. We encourage participants to let their expression flow. Often, however, the emerging image contains a sense of order or balance that can reflect the new internal state. A mandala created by a participant can be used at home as a focal point, as a reminder of connection with self.

Mandala creation has been shown to support mental health and well-being (e.g., Babouchkina, & Robbins, 2015; Kima, Kima, Choeb, & Kimb, 2018; Pisarik, & Larson, 2011). There is reliable evidence that colouring in mandala designs can improve mood (e.g., Curry & Kasser, 2005; Van der Vennet & Serice, 2012). Mandala drawing has been used to support cognitive, socio-emotional and spiritual integration (Young, 2001). When mandala drawing was used as an activity for children diagnosed with ADD and ADHD, the drawing increased the children's ability to pay attention and decreased impulsive behaviours (Smitheman-Brown & Church, 1996).

In Western psychotherapeutic practice, the use of the mandala was introduced by Jung (1973), who observed that clients became calmer when expressing in a circular frame.

Mandalas are useful as outer expressions of an inner experience. How the mandala appears to others, or the creator's drawing skills, are not important. It is the process of expression via mandala creation that assists integration.

It is ideal to create a mandala image immediately after an activity, before too much verbal sharing, while contact with the internal experience is available and present. There is no need for a participant to interpret a mandala, simply allow the creative experience to nourish and inform.

It is very important that we never interpret or project our own ideas onto a participant's artistic expression. While we may think we see something in another's creation, each person must be afforded the time and right to find their own meaning.

Preparing several circles in advance of an activity can assist participants to gain more freedom in drawing. Use a light pencil to create a perfect circle, e.g., draw around a plate, or invite the participant to quickly create a freehand circle. Also, as a support to gaining more freedom with the drawing process, it can be useful at times to try drawing with the non-dominant hand (see page 34). Participants can be invited to relax and listen to different types of music, then let their hand and crayons take over and quickly express any feeling response to the music.

A Note on Group Work

Using the activities in this book with groups can add a valuable social, interactive component that increases skills development. Groups with the aim to address behaviour problems, grief and loss, and socialisation issues are often found in schools, community counselling centres, and are conducted through private practices. The focus of a personal development group can be determined by the members' interests and needs; however, groups designed to develop emotional resilience; deal with grief, loss and separation; support family transitions, or address behavioural problems can be useful. There are many research studies that have shown positive outcomes from the use of expressive arts in group work with young people, but it is not possible to list them all here. However, we will highlight a few.

Sosin, Noble, Harrichand, and Bohecker (2022) found that creative and expressive arts group activities gave members insight into current coping behaviours and validated their sense of self. They also noted that group leaders' qualities, and the relationship they facilitated between group members, were critical to the effectiveness of a creative arts, personal growth group (Sosin, Noble, Harrichand, & Bohecker, 2022), and this reminds us that it is the people guiding and participating in groups, the relationships, that remain central to positive outcomes.

When working with groups of young people, the recommended ideal group size is 3–6 for younger children, 5–7 children for ages 6–9, and up to 8 children in preteen and teen groups (DeLucia-Waack, 2006, p.19).

Groups provide opportunities for young clients to develop and practice interactional and communication skills, and creative arts groups have been shown to increase empathy among group members (e.g., Cain, 2019 and 2023). Groups provide opportunities for members to give feedback to each other on the impact of their behaviour, ideally in a positive way, which may contribute to members experiencing feelings of acceptance, trust and being helped. Having opportunities to learn to accept, trust and help others is another advantage. Group members can learn to deal with fears related to hopes of inclusion and fears of exclusion. Leading a discussion in a sub-group can begin to nurture some leadership skills, and overall, members have the opportunity to normalise their experience as they discover what is happening "under the surface" for others.

A sense of playfulness can emerge within group work that supports relaxation in the activities. Holm-Hadulla and Hofmann (2012) described the way playful explorations of problems and conflicts can lead to new and useful insights and emotional awareness. Playful curiosity has also been identified as a key factor in generating creativity (Csikszentmihalyi, 1997). Experiences centred in creativity and the arts may hold promise for increased well-being of future generations (Nathan, 2019).

There are many challenges in conducting group work with young clients. An ideal approach in the implementation of Expressive Therapies activities is the person-centred relational style of the group leader. Person-centred group leaders show concern and respect for the subjective experience of each participant. Corey (2008) identified themes of person-centred group leadership, including the importance of supporting growth in one's own and participants' self-awareness, commitment to a developing reflective ability, striving to understand reality from the client's perspective and trust in the self-actualisation tendency (Maslow, 1962). An essential belief from a person-centred leader is that participants are essentially self-determining beings and group processes can support their freedom to make productive choices.

Practicalities for Group Presenters

- If working with a group, it is ideal to have two facilitators: one to keep contact with the whole group, one to attend to or encourage individuals when needed.
- Always work with the activities yourself, experience them, before presenting. This will increase confidence, which can be sensed by participants.
- Before presenting, review the exercise carefully. Is the language appropriate for the age group you are working with, and for their cultural backgrounds?
- Set up the space, bring order into the work-space, before beginning – preferably before participants come in. Check that you have any materials needed before beginning.
- Ideally, the light should be gentle. Close curtains or blinds, dim lights, so that their eyes can relax. This also helps the focus be turned within, there is less connection to, and distraction from, the outside world.
- Make sure the work-space is:
    - delineated – e.g., cushions or chairs can set the boundary if working in a large area.
    - ordered – order, tidiness and beautiful impressions help to make the space psychologically safe.
- Give a brief overview of the aim and sequence of the activity before presenting.
- Always repeat your instructions at least twice. Look carefully to see if you have been understood. Do you need to rephrase the instruction?
- If using background music, always check its suitability first. Turn it down as you give instructions. Fade it in and out gently.
- When inviting participants to step back from outer focus by closing their eyes, always add a brief rationale.
- Make it clear at each stage whether participants' eyes are best open or closed, and when you want them to look at you, relate to each other, or stay focused within.
- If you sense resistance in participants, invite them to talk about it, help them understand any hesitation, before beginning. This decreases its impact.

- Stay sensitive and flexible with time. Watch attention spans. Give time boundaries clearly, and give time warnings when it is nearly time to stop an activity or a section of it.
- Talk to the participants about the idea of confidentiality during the debriefing discussions with each other.
- A simple way to evaluate outcomes after an activity is to have the participants write down some words or phrases "which best describe their responses to the activities". The responses are likely to give the presenter confidence to proceed.

Working as part of a group can develop peer support skills, peer permission and acceptance for expression. Participants in a group can feel a reduction in the sense of isolation and aloneness with their concerns. They can develop new and deeper empathic connections that can carry over after group times. A sense of playfulness can emerge in group work that supports relaxation in the activities. As participants expand their self-awareness, as an outcome of engaging with the activities, this can also increase their acceptance and awareness of inter-personal differences. Some participants, new to working in a group, may experience feelings of acceptance for the first time, and this can contribute to increases in self-acceptance.

Developing a Stronger Sense of Self with Group Participants

- Accept a participant's present feelings. Give space for them to be heard. Then, help them come back to themselves, and focus on body, feeling and thoughts.
- Develop body awareness – this is basic to a strong sense of self. Use the activities in this book: relaxation, mindfulness, body movement, breathing exercises and visualisation.
- Treat participants with respect, model this and insist they relate to each other respectfully.
- As a presenter, seek opportunities to provide participants with specific encouragement. If criticism is necessary, be specific.
- Give them responsibilities, independence and the freedom to make choices.
- Allow them to experiment, pursue their own ways of participating and expressing, to be creative or not creative.
- Avoid being judgemental – whether it is positive or negative.

Creating Positive Group Dynamics

- Provide safety, structure, support and flexibility
- Provide freedom of expression

- Develop trust and a bond as the first step to a successful group
- Acknowledge that everyone has a story or important experience
- Make it safe for everyone to communicate and express differently
- Accept that everyone has a different level of comfort with self-revelation
- Give permission for each group member to process reactions to an activity, or to other group members, in private, without offending others
- Model respect for differences
- Model respect for participants' readiness or resistance to communicate
- Model sharing of positive responses
- Find support and/or supervision to deal with any less-than-positive emotional responses.

Sharing Experience during Group Sessions

Discuss these guidelines for times of debriefing after activities:

- Make an effort to listen, allow others in the group time to share
- Never interrupt or chat while others have the focus of the group
- Comment on what someone shares only if they have asked for feedback
- Don't tell anyone what to think or feel
- Aim to point out how well others are doing
- If you are unhappy about anything, talk to the presenter about it
- You don't have to share your experience
- Don't use any "put-downs" – can you use "build-ups"?
- Keep private what others share. Don't talk about what people do or say in the group.

A Language for the Inner World

Symbols and imagery are often called the language of the imagination. Imagination is partly an expression of unconscious processes. Artists, designers, composers and scientists, those who make creative leaps in their work, use their imagination. Each of us has creative potential. The activities in this book

> *The therapist's role is an important one in group settings.*
>
> *She must set the tone of the group as a place where children can feel safe and accepted.*
>
> *A certain amount of modelling must take place; children take their cues from the therapist.*
>
> *A satisfactory group session is one in which each child feels interested, interesting, safe and accepted.*
>
> (Oaklander, 1978)

are designed to help participants tap into that creative potential. They also support participants to take note of the images or fragments of fantasies that contain expressions of their inner world. Taking note of the inner world will also support self-esteem. Activities using visualisations can generate creativity, enthusiasm for creative writing, art, drama and personal development.

Symbols provide an extended language for understanding and expressing subtle experiences, sensations, emotions and realisations. Symbols and imagery are fluid, expansive and not limited by set rational meanings as words so often are.

Just as a toddler feels relief when language becomes effective, participants experience satisfaction and fulfilment when subtle areas of their inner world find new ways to be recognised and communicated. Using symbols and imagery contributes to the process of recognition and communication of the strengths, feelings, ideas, directions that in many of us can remain out of sight, ignored, in favour of intellectual pursuits.

There is an in-built mechanism that orientates our psyche towards wholeness. In order to be re-owned, the disconnected parts of our psyche often appear as symbols in dreams, fantasies and in visualisations. These symbols can be of positive aspects, such as talents, courage and the ability to care, or of emotions seeking recognition. Pondering the meaning of a symbol that has been presented from within – even imagining ourselves becoming a symbol through role-play – can advance reconnection with the inner world.

Symbols that hold psychological significance can appear during visualisations. Direct symbol interpretation by another person is not useful. Individuals need to feel and understand symbolic meanings within themselves.

Guided Mental Imagery and Visualisation

Encouraging visualisation provides ways for clients to focus and actively use imagination, to develop more positive relationships to self and the world. Visualisation activities can be directed, given boundaries, or free form, with lots of silence for participants to follow their own internal imagery. Using imagery, metaphor and guided visualisation have a long history as tools for insight in therapy (Jacobs, 1990). It has been well documented that mental imagery can elicit strong emotional responses (Holmes et al., 2008; Holmes & Matthews, 2010). Guided visualisation of positive scenarios, positive memories and positive emotions has been found to lift mood, to increase positive affect (Knagg, Pratt, Taylor, & Palmier-Claus, 2021).

Self-reassurance is associated with ease and clarity of generating warm and supportive images of the self (Gilbert et al., 2006). Difficulties in generating self-reassurance and compassionate images about self may also contribute to depressive symptoms. People can cope better with failures if they have access to a warm, supportive schema of self and/or others. The degree to which people are able to access warm and supportive, or condemning and critical, other-to-self and self-to-self scripts and memories has a central bearing on emotional and social responses to events. Gilbert and Irons (2004) explored how teaching people to generate self-soothing, compassionate and warm images for the self could act as an antidote for harsh self-critical tendencies.

Some visualisation activities guide participants on a journey of imagination that brings them to a threshold, an imaginary or a remembered real place that becomes familiar during the activity. It is usually a natural, safe, beautiful place and is used as a doorway into the realm of their own imagination. The journey part of visualisations prepares a clear space in participants' minds for the imagination to freely create. Asking participants to use their own imagination, the presenter directs them to explore beyond the threshold of the given story. This prepares a space for their own symbolic thinking, imagery and stories to emerge. Then, they are guided to return to the starting point, bringing new imagery or insight with them.

Visualisations work well with groups and individuals. They help participants connect to positive perspectives about themselves. It may be very supportive for younger children to invite them to describe their discoveries to you, as they find them, or in group work, to a partner who simply listens. This helps them stay in touch with an imagined journey. Sometimes participants could draw during the visualisation. However, lying down with eyes closed may assist deeper engagement. Quiet music can be used to set the mood.

Some Typical Stages in Visualisation Journeys

- Present an overview of the activity and a rationale for doing it
- Begin with some relaxation, centring and/or body awareness
- Describe a safe, beautiful setting, involving the senses in the descriptions
- Describe a threshold that the story has led to, e.g., a gate, a clearing in the forest
- Allow an open space and time for the imagination to generate its own extension of the story with symbols, images and story
- Return to the threshold place
- Visualise the journey back to the starting point, retracing their steps
- Return awareness to the here and now, the outer reality
- Record symbols, images, gifts, words of wisdom, etc.
- Debrief through discussion about the experience
- Explore any relevance of the images to the participant's life

Visualisation can harness images from the unconscious, from dreams, fairy tales, as well as universal symbols, including popular heroes/heroines from contemporary culture. Visualisations can explore themes of discovery of treasure and inner strength, inner stillness and resolution of conflicts, and can set the scene for self-guidance and clarity.

Inviting discussion of any artwork created after visualisation journeys may reveal what is happening in the inner world. These discussions can help a presenter trace the development of self-awareness, a sense of self, and ability with increased access to the imaginative realm.

For very active young participants, preparatory activities that alternate tensing and relaxing the body will be helpful towards being able to be still enough to close eyes and allow internal focus.

Of course, not everyone can be fluent with metal imagery or visualisation. Aphantasia is an inability to visualise. Otherwise known as *image-free thinking*. People with aphantasia can't create a mental image, e.g., of familiar objects, people, or places or images of the future (Aphantasia Network). Dance, Ipser and Simner (2022) found that there is a prevalence of aphantasia in the general population of 3.9%. This means, for participation in visualisations, it is ideal to have a set of miniatures that the client can select and arrange, rather than holding or developing an image in their mind.

Reducing Participants' Self-criticism

Many of us share the challenge of dealing with habitual self-criticism. Sadly, it is a widespread habit globally. A self-critical voice – or self – evolves in the hope that one can change, and therefore achieve, whatever has been needed from significant others in early years. Pervasive self-criticism can be likened to a script, a self or perhaps even a "voice", scolding from the inside – imposing rules about what individuals do, need, and can feel, and who they can be. Developed earlier in life, the inner critic absorbs expectations of family and society, then mimics judgements towards self that originated from significant others. Unconsciously, an internal feedback loop can continue throughout life, sabotaging confidence. Out of this process evolves a pattern in the personality, a cognitive schema, collectively named the inner critic, which endlessly aims to correct and scold from within (Pearson & Wilson, 2024).

Raising the topic of self-criticism, helping our participants recognise any such tendency, and providing antidotes such as mindful self-compassion practice (see page 104), can be valuable for people of all ages. For example, Compassion-Focused Therapy (Gilbert et al., 2004) was developed to help people who experience self-criticism and shame to soften their harsh criticism. In CBT, clients are invited to make a study of their negative self-talk as a first step in gaining freedom. Grounding, self-awareness, mindfulness and self-compassion – the background aims of the activities in this book – are also antidotes and support a person to have some distance from this intrusive tendency.

In presenting the activities in this book, it is essential to work with a "participants can't get it wrong" approach. We aim to avoid creating experiences that could provide fodder for the inner critic. It can be so helpful for our participants if we make comments such as "There is no right or wrong way to do this" and "It is your experiment. See how you would like to do it".

Using Positive Memory and Mental Imagery

A pioneer in positive psychology was Martin Seligman (2002). He aimed to shift focus in psychology from pathology to flourishing and happiness. Positive psychology emphasises strengths, gratitude and optimism, fostering personal and societal growth. Positive psychology focuses on building skills and the development of positive emotions that can be channelled towards prevention, treatment and coping with problems (Fredrickson, 2001).

Since 2001, positive writing has included reflecting on and writing about happiness, self-actualisation, deepening experiences of satisfaction, gratitude, awe and well-being. A very recent meta-analysis of the research literature has shown that positive reflection and writing are beneficial (Hoult, Wetherell, Edginton, & Smith, 2025), and in particular writing interventions about our "best possible self" and gratitude revealed the most consistent benefits. Gratitude helps to increase satisfaction with life because it highlights the good memories about the past, which can lead to greater life satisfaction. So, increasing the gratitude for the good aspects of the past intensifies the positive memories (Li, Zhu, Li, & Cui, 2023).

A Discussion on Relaxation

Various types of relaxation are represented among the activities in this book, such as progressive relaxation (similar to Jacobson's sequential contraction and relaxation of major muscle groups [1929, cited in Lusebrink, 1990]) and use of imagery – e.g., a rag doll and melting cheese on a pizza (similar to Schultz's Autogenic Training which uses images of warmth and heaviness to invoke relaxation [in Lusebrink. 1990]). The importance of the "let it happen" attitude to relaxation and the passive concentration on the breathing recommended by Schultz in Autogenic Training (Benson & Klipper, 2000) also reflects the approach to relaxation adopted here.

Relaxation can be used as a basis for also developing sensory awareness and has proved useful in supporting clients' therapeutic process. Relaxation is introduced to clients to enhance their self-care skills base and is used in therapy sessions as an integration process, particularly after expressive work with emotions.

Relaxation training has proved useful over time in many fields of endeavour (Carlson & Hoyle, 1993; Goldfried & Trier, 1974; Ost, 1987). Biophysical methods using muscle relaxation have added to the success of cognitive-behavioural approaches for many years (Rosenberg, Wilson, Maheady, & Sindelar, 1997). Relaxation therapy is evidence-based and was found to be efficacious, non-invasive and cost-efficient (Lovas, 2015). Lovas' review of the research highlighted that relaxation can maintain health and well-being amid the rapid change and chronic stress of today's society.

Relaxation is a practical skill that needs to be performed regularly to be effective (Lovas, 2015). Lovas (2015) reported that relaxation training improved sleep quality and cognitive function in people aged 60 years or older, and anxiety was reduced by relaxation techniques in hospitalised patients and people with cancer. Depression was reduced in caregivers, in women challenged by breast cancer, people with chronic fatigue, post-traumatic stress disorder and adolescent psychiatric patients. Relaxation reduced nightmares, depression, sleep disturbances and dissociation in trauma-exposed individuals and improved post-surgical wound healing.

Benson and Klipper (2000) refer to the extensive medical research on the value of relaxation and describe the inherent relaxation response as an "innate mechanism within us". The key ingredients that support this relaxation response are a quiet environment, the use of a mental device, a passive attitude towards allowing the body to relax and a physically comfortable position.

Holian (2001) found the use of ET creative visualisations highly effective as an adjunct in supporting student relaxation, as well as increasing concentration. A school-based relaxation training programme reduced students' stress and anxiety levels and can be used as a preventative strategy (Morton & Cescato, 2000). Research results revealed a significant reduction in stress for university students, with medium to large effect sizes during their first visit to participate in a self-guided relaxation zone programme (Jones et al., 2023).

Autogenic Relaxation Training (self-directed use of relaxation imagery) has proved to be effective in reducing anxiety and depression in some health conditions (Vasu et al., 2020). It was beneficial in reducing anxiety and depression, and improving functional ability, mobility and quality of life among stroke survivors. Relaxation therapy is effective in reducing PTSD severity, anxiety and depression symptoms, and to improve quality of life (Carletto et al., 2016).

Music-assisted relaxation can lower the systolic blood pressure of patients with diabetes and a comorbidity of hypertension (Mandel, Davis, & Secic, 2013). The level of students' anxiety when facing a test was decreased after participating in group counselling activities with relaxation techniques, assisted by music (Nurlela & Jannati, 2019).

A Discussion on Mindfulness

Mindfulness practice has been shown to lead to increases in well-being and therapeutic presence when we are supporting others. Mindfulness emphasises the importance of experience over knowledge and focuses very much on generating non-judgemental awareness in the here and now. Mindfulness practice has implications for both integration in therapy and for personal and spiritual exploration through focused attention. The content of what is observed during mindful practice – especially our thoughts – always contains some magnetic pull to draw us in to replaying the emotional, somatic or cognitive content, ruminating on it until it dominates the foreground. The key is to maintain the position of the observer rather than identify with the content (Pearson & Wilson, 2009).

Also, for us, being self-aware, attempting our own mindfulness practice, while offering support to others, increases our self-care, can provide a model of calm focus, and helps a client experience our presence and support. Mindfulness is "paying attention in a particular way: on purpose, in the present moment, and nonjudgmentally" (Kabat-Zinn, 1994, p. 4) and "awareness of present experience with acceptance" (Germer, 2005, p. 7). Mindfulness is a term with varying definitions, being used more frequently in the therapeutic and psychological literature. Mindfulness has become popular among therapists, and mindfulness practice has implications for effective integration of the therapy process. Focusing attention internally is claimed to provide building blocks for new neural pathways (Siegel, 2007), and such neural rebuilding is an indicator that therapy has supported fundamental change.

Several of the activities in this book have evolved from working with the Mindfulness-based Cognitive Therapy (MBCT) programme activities. This programme was developed for depressed adults in the 1990s by Segal, Williams and Teasdale (2012). The MBCT programme evolved from the Mindfulness-based Stress Reduction (MBSR) model pioneered by Jon Kabat-Zinn (which has a strong evidence base). MBSR embraces the practice of mindfulness and "being with" experience, rather than adjusting, judging or controlling experience. It aims to help participants disengage from the automatic "doing" mode and to access a decentred "being" mode of mind (Felder, Dimidjian, & Segal, 2012).

Hinterkopf (1998) recommended a mindful focusing activity to support therapy clients to reconnect with their spirituality; a simple process that can activate individual existential search. This, in turn, can generate new experiences of meaning and personal satisfaction – which have been shown to contribute to resilience.

Pointing out that mindfulness has been in use in Western psychotherapeutic practice since the 1970s, Whitfield (2006) described mindfulness as supporting dis-identification with internal experiences. A client would be encouraged to observe the present moment and recognise a thought as simply a thought, and not be enticed into identifying with it or following inner experiences to the point where they could become persuasive and convincing. In perceiving cognitive, emotional and somatic events more closely, the client may be able to reduce reactive tendencies – one of the aims of traditional meditation. Promoting mindfulness in therapists has an influence on the treatment results of their clients (Grepmair et al., 2007). Therapists in training who participated in a mindfulness meditation course had significantly higher evaluations for individual therapy on scales related to clarification and problem-solving perspectives (Grepmair et al., 2007). The clients of the therapist group that practised meditation showed greater symptom reduction than those working with the therapists in training who did not practice meditation. Additionally, a short programme of mindfulness meditation produced observable effects on brain and immune function (Davidson et al., 2003), suggesting that meditation may change brain and immune function in positive ways and that mindfulness practice ought to be mandatory for counselling interns, and a ready option in providing support.

Although most of us who wish to work with young people will be focusing on what we DO, it seems that children learn most from what we ARE. It is of little use to teach them meditation or relaxation if we are not at the same time connected to some form of meditative or self-aware practice, and moving towards a more relaxed and open state. An important aspect of our preparation to support others is to clear any of our own reactivity, to come to a fuller connection with ourselves. Working towards all this, and offering support from this state of knowledge, will provide a direct model for clients.

"Beginner's mind" is a familiar expression in the Zen tradition (Goodman, 2013). It encompasses qualities of openness, receptiveness, and readiness to learn. Mindfulness practice cultivates the states of openness and relaxed spontaneity into which beginners in life are born. Therapists may need to bridge a natural, cultural divide (adulthood to childhood) to connect. Beginner's mind can help the therapist enter into the world of the young person.

Our own beginner's mind can be a gift to children. When we are in this state, they are then free to come forward and experience our relaxed space of receptivity. Our peaceful state of being invites children to "come as they are", with self-acceptance. Children are more likely than adults to live in the present moment – they are often confused by adult conceptions of time and sequence. Children are very sensitive to acceptance or disapproval by others. The aspect of mindfulness that is non-judgemental, accepting of what is, creates a necessary atmosphere of emotional safety and trustworthiness in the consulting room. The parallels here with Rogers' (2051) person-centred approach to counselling are obvious

The first two chapters of activities in this book seek to introduce the components of mindfulness practice in a playful way. Some focus on breath, some focus on directing attention, and some build in the development of somatic and sensory awareness, with an overall direction towards building present moment awareness. It is essential to welcome the sharing of observations of mind-wandering, reinforce that this is normal and bring acceptance to what is observed, while also encouraging refreshed efforts to return to focused attention.

Mindfulness activities for young people are designed to help them cultivate some stability and flexibility of attention. In many activities, relaxation comes first to release excess tension in the body and mind. Then, the cultivation of mindful awareness by focusing on one of our physical senses, focusing externally and then internally. Practising the activities can lessen distraction and absentmindedness, and enhance clarity of awareness.

Regular mindfulness practice can cultivate three core skills: concentration – the ability to focus and stabilise one's attention; sensory clarity – the ability to keep track of the components of sensory experience as they arise in various combinations, moment-by-moment; and equanimity – the ability to "be with" experience with an attitude of gentle acceptance and non-judgement.

Contraindications for Using Mindfulness

If clients are unable to adequately concentrate on activities, or where paying attention to the activity appears overly taxing from the very start, do not proceed with activities that require focus. Start with movement and breathing games that also engage imagination.

A few suggestions about when to avoid mindfulness practice:

- If the participant appears to have a significant learning disability
- If the participant seems uninterested or unprepared to invest time in the activities
- If the participant's socioeconomic/living circumstances require immediate attention (e.g., danger, pending eviction, overwhelming financial debt, legal actions)
- If there appears to be a problem with proficiency in the spoken language
- If the participant appears to be dealing with significant mental health problems
- Those in early phases of PTSD, where they are not able to focus on current experience
- If the participant has shown signs of being overwhelmed by rumination
- Traumatised participants who experience flashbacks
- If a participant has unrealistic expectations about mindfulness outcomes
- If you do not have personal and professional experience with mindfulness and clinical work

Offering Advice on Developing a Mindfulness Practice

The author's research (Pearson, 2019) applied thematic analysis to written reports from 53 post-graduate counselling interns who participated in piloting an eight-week mindfulness challenge, since the personal development of a counsellor is core to therapy outcomes. The findings showed that mindfulness could be practised through a variety of activities, leading to observations of self, insights about self and insights about mindfulness practice. The interns' reports indicated that mindfulness was not easy to learn, and for most, the practice contributed to growth in self-awareness. The most often stated advice for beginners in mindfulness practice was to find a way to practice that they enjoyed and that "worked for them". Categories of advice included advice about starting practice, about letting go of expectations, about outcomes and benefits and a few practical tips.

Advice offered for those about to start a mindfulness practice included: "Identify the methods of practice you enjoy and work for you", "It does require effort and commitment" and "Have a plan and be persistent despite challenges". One intern stated that "a kind and gentle curiosity is needed". Letting go of expectations was a repeated recommendation, for example: "Don't expect instant miracles", "It is not an exercise that requires perfection", "Start small" and "Challenges should be expected".

Five statements that summarised key advice that emerged from the interns' experience also indicated that they had begun to understand the elusive nature of focused attention: "It is not as easy as it seems, and results are not immediate", "Thoughts are always going to come", "Relapse (into non-practice) is natural", "See it as a journey not a goal to achieve" and "There is no right or wrong way to do mindfulness".

Tips on Introducing Mindfulness Practice

- First engage a client's interest in self-discovery vs self-change
- Success in connecting with "how it is inside" is success in mindfulness
- Provide options and alternatives – emphasise that it is a self-experiment
- Try to offer questions, not issue commands, in order to make it safe around arousing failure
- Mindfulness practice is "on purpose"; make sure the purpose is clear
- A group setting can add to the normalisation and validation that we all have obstacles to mindfulness efforts
- Practice saying: "It's your experiment" and "There is no right or wrong way".

Creative Expression after Mindfulness Practice

After a mindfulness activity, invite participants to engage in creative expression about their experience. This can support consolidation, integration and meaning-making. Spontaneous expression via colours and lines, drawing on body outlines, mandala circles (see more on pages 34 and 35), writing, using clay or arranging miniatures, can all be very helpful for a client to integrate and transition from inner-world experience to the outer world. For some, there may be no words to describe their experience, so the creative arts non-verbal approach is recommended.

Invite clients to express creatively after an activity:

- *Let it be spontaneous*
- *Try not to think about it too much*
- *See what colours you are drawn to*
- *Are there shapes that your hand would like to make?*
- *Is there an image in your mind you would like to capture on paper?*
- *Let yourself play and experiment*
- *There is no correct way to create; it is your time to play and experiment*

Mindfulness Activity Skills Checklist

For use when creating your own mindfulness activities,

Which of these would be most useful for your participants?
In what order could these best be introduced?

- Finding creative and playful activities that lead to relaxation
- Finding motivation for self-focus
- Ability to move, stretch and tense the body in a way that leads to relaxation
- Creating a space and time for stillness without interruptions
- Surrendering any expectations, agendas, struggles or goals
- Releasing surface frustrations
- Finding a balanced posture for meditation

- Ability to repeatedly return the focus of non-judgemental awareness to:
    - body sensation
    - breath
    - emotional state
    - thoughts
    - energy
- Aiming for a compassionate state towards self – letting go of self-criticism
- Developing discipline with returning awareness to the present moment
- Ability to divide attention between internal experiences and the outside world
- Ability to use visualisation for relaxation and connection with spiritual impulse
- Cultivating an attitude of relaxation and meditation of surrender – "letting it happen"
- Integration and recording of experiences – writing, drawing and discussion

Mindfulness in Nature and Trauma Support

In Chapter 4, in particular, and elsewhere in the activities, there are invitations to imagine or recall times in nature. While the evidence is now strong for the well-being outcomes associated with time in nature (e.g. Russell et al., 2013), there is also evidence for positive benefits from psychological connection with nature (Barragan-Jason et al., 2023).

If you feel inspired to create your own visualisations for supporting relaxation and internal focus, consider settings that feel safe and beautiful. It may be helpful with young participants to invite them to picture a place in nature they know well, for example, a beach, lagoon, lake, grandparents' garden or favourite park.

Over the last 20 years, there has been rapid growth in understanding the needs of traumatised young clients, and in the evidence of the contribution of creative arts therapies in positive therapeutic outcomes (e.g., Carey, 2006; Malchiodi, 2020; Perry, 2006; van Westrhenen et al., 2017). Expressive arts approaches effectively treat trauma (e.g., Sosin, Noble, Harrichand, & Bohecker, 2022). Creative and expressive arts techniques facilitate understanding and expression of implicit aspects of trauma memories that are challenging to tolerate and put into words. Additionally, a mindfulness approach adds to increased cognitive flexibility and emotional and physiological regulation in response to trauma activation (Strand & Stige, 2021).

If supporting young people who have experienced trauma, it is recommended (e.g., by Rothschild, 2010) that early in the interactions, a safe place is established in the mind of the person, and shared with the presenter of the activities. Return to visualising this safe place can then be used as an antidote to emotional overwhelm, and an activity that can "put the brakes on" when needed. See preparation activity on page 29.

A Discussion on Self-compassion

Most of us live in cultures that do not emphasise self-compassion, quite the opposite. We are told that we're being lazy and self-indulgent if we don't harshly criticise ourselves. We are told – or it is implied – that no matter how hard we try, our best is not good enough.

Self-compassion, as conceptualised by Neff (2003) and Gilbert (2009), has drawn on traditions from Buddhist concepts and practices as well as the construct of social psychology (Karris & Caldwell, 2015). The capacity to be self-compassionate has been identified as useful to promote personal well-being and has been identified as beneficial for both intra- and inter-personal relating (Neff & Vonk, 2009). It has been associated with a reduction in anxiety and rumination, increased social relatedness and enhanced life satisfaction (Neff, Kirkpatrick, & Rude, 2007).

Self-compassion has three main components: Acknowledging a moment of suffering – staying present to it; feeling that it is part of being human, a shared human experience; and expressing kindness to self (Neff, 2003). Neff tells us that self-compassion entails being warm and understanding towards ourselves when we suffer, fail or feel inadequate, rather than ignoring our pain or responding with harsh self-criticism. Self-compassionate people recognise that being imperfect, failing and experiencing life difficulties is inevitable, so they tend to be gentle with themselves when confronted with painful experiences rather than getting angry when life falls short.

Self-compassion involves recognising that suffering and personal inadequacy are part of the shared human experience – something that we all go through rather than being something that happens to "me" alone. It also stems from the willingness to observe our negative thoughts and emotions with openness and clarity, so that they are held in mindful awareness. Mindfulness is a non-judgemental, receptive mind state in which one observes thoughts and feelings as they are, without trying to suppress or deny them. Neff cautions that we cannot ignore our pain and feel compassion for it at the same time.

Neff (2003) found that self-compassion practice led to acceptance of thoughts without judgement, a softening of self-criticism, buffering against negative self-feelings, reduced negative reactions, and prevented being overwhelmed with negative emotions. Research findings have clearly indicated that kindness to self, the capacity to tolerate difficult feelings without over-identification with those feelings and embracing a "bigger picture" perspective of life challenges can be a "powerful predictor of mental health" (Neff, Kirkpatrick, & Rude, 2007, p. 909).

It is vital that therapists encouraging self-compassion practice with their clients be aware of the phenomenon of backdraft. This is one reason that, for some clients, self-compassion practice can make them feel worse. When the door of the heart is opened with compassion, intense pain can sometimes be released (Gilbert, McEwan, Matos, & Rivis, 2011). Providing ourselves with unconditional love may reveal or awaken the conditions under which we felt unloved in the past. Therefore, some clients, especially those with a history of childhood abuse or neglect, are fearful of compassion (Gilbert, McEwan, Matos, & Rivis, 2011).

Harvard psychologist Christopher Germer (2009) suggests that there are five ways to bring self-compassion into our lives: via physical, mental, emotional, relational and spiritual methods. These are a few ways to encourage more self-compassion in life:

- Comfort your body
    - Eat something healthy
    - Lie down and rest your body
    - Massage your own neck, feet or hands
    - Take a walk
    - Anything you can do to improve how you feel physically gives you a dose of self-compassion
- Write a letter to yourself. Describe a situation that caused you to feel pain (a breakup with a lover, a job loss, a poorly received presentation)
    - Don't blame anyone but acknowledge your feelings
- Give yourself encouragement
    - If something bad or painful happens to you, think of what you would say to a good friend if the same thing happened to him or her
    - Direct these compassionate responses towards yourself
- Practice mindfulness
    - This is the non-judgemental observation of your own thoughts, feelings and actions, without trying to suppress or deny them
    - When you look in the mirror and don't like what you see, accept the bad with the good with a compassionate attitude.

2 Preparation and Rapport-Building Activities

Creating Safety; Supporting Freedom with Art and Writing

Activities in this chapter are designed to build a sense of safety for participants. They also support participants to become familiar with ways of integrating experiences, artistically expressing their responses and reflecting on their experience as they engage with the activities in the following chapters. Some activities are particularly effective for building participant connections when working with groups.

Some of the background components of activities are explored to enable familiarisation in a way that these components do not seem to be unusual or strange or, as some young ones say, "weird". These components include taking deeper breaths, recognising differences between self-criticism and self-kindness, breaking free in visual art expressions, reviewing the impact of activities, getting to know group members and exploring somatic awareness.

DOI: 10.4324/9781003716501-2

SAFETY VISUALISATION

My Safe and Beautiful Place in Nature

Tune in to your inner self, your body and feelings and thoughts. Take a deep breath, and relax it out. See if you can relax your whole body a little. See if you can remember or imagine a beautiful, safe area in nature which attracts you, a place you love to be. This is a place with some beauty, where you feel safe and happy. See if you could let a picture or memory form in your mind. It could be a real place, or it could be a place you make up in your mind.

It could be, for example, a favourite beach, in the mountains, by a creek, or in a park, or

- *it may be a place where you can see the sky, trees, flowers, beautiful views;*
- *it could be a special part of your garden at home or at a friend's place.*

Could you imagine being at this beautiful place in nature?

- *What are the main things you would see? Imagine looking up, down, from side to side.*
- *What would you see, hear? smell? Touch with your hands? Imagine you are there now.*
- *What would be your main feelings while you are in this place?*

See if you could imagine moving through this place:

- *Become interested in the details of what you remember, what you see in your mind.*
- *Is there anyone there with you?*
- *Take time and allow the pictures to soak in, enjoy them.* (pause)
- *Is there anything that stands out for you? Anything that is most noticeable in this place, that catches your attention?*

When you are ready, move to the art paper and crayons, and see if you could do a quick sketch of the main things you remember, or some parts of that beautiful place. It doesn't matter if you are good at drawing or not. Just quickly sketch something that will remind you of the place.

If it helps to capture the feeling of this place, you could write down a few words around the picture. (pause while they draw)

Would you like to share your sketch?

- *Would you like to talk a little about what you have drawn?*
- *How did you feel about being there?*
- *If you gave your picture a title, what would it be?*

USING BREATH TO SUPPORT OPENING UP

Ways to Take Deep Breaths

When we want to understand ourselves and explore activities that help us relax, taking some deep breaths can help. When we take in a deep breath, then relax it out, it can energise our ability to focus and connect with our thoughts, feelings and body.

This activity offers three breathing games to help you get used to playful ways of taking deep breaths.

1. *Firstly, could you pretend to be a whale coming to the surface of the ocean and exhaling powerfully? Imagine a fine spray of water bursting out. Then, take in a huge amount of air, hold it, imagine diving down deep, then surfacing again and letting it all out until you are empty. Could you try this a few times?* (repeat)
2. *For the next game, you might like to stand up and have a stretch. Now, could you imagine that you have become a magnificent fire-breathing dragon? Feel how tall and strong you are. You have arrived at the fire-breathing dragon championship competition. There are champion dragons of all sizes, shapes and ages, gathered from all around the world. On the count of three, we will see who can send their flames across the greatest distance. Take a huge breath in, and hold it. One, two, three: let the flames loose! Shall we try again?* (repeat)
3. *For the next game, could you imagine that you are a very large balloon? You are a self-inflating balloon, one that blows itself up. It will take you three big breaths to be stretched as full as can be. Here we go: first breath in, hold it, now add the second breath in, now the third! Now let it all out with a big noise! Great! Let's try it a few times.* (repeat)

Now take a moment to rest.

How do you feel now after the breathing games?

EXPLORING SELF-TALK HABITS

Discussing Criticism and Self-kindness

Showing care and support to others helps us strengthen friendships. Being kind to others also helps us feel good. At the same time, we all need self-kindness. Many people notice that they can be kind to others, but quite critical towards themselves. This can make them feel down, feel sad and a bit depressed. Sometimes criticising ourselves seems like a habit that we don't notice. This discussion activity can help you notice more often ways we think and feel about ourselves.

This short discussion activity can help us get clear on what is self-criticism, and what is self-kindness or self-compassion.

Can you tell which of these statements are self-criticism, and which show self-kindness?

1. *I took a break from homework to jump on the trampoline.*
2. *I'm annoyed with myself that I didn't get everything done. I must be too lazy.*
3. *I really should have practised more. I really messed this up, as usual.*
4. *I did a fantastic job cleaning up my room. I can play and enjoy it now.*
5. *I don't feel confident in drawing, but I'm happy to have a go.*
6. *I know most people worry about things, so I try not to worry about worrying.*

Now, let's practise remembering some positives about yourself over the last week or two, that could bring alive our self-kindness:

- *Is there something you are proud of yourself for recently?*
- *Was there something over the last few weeks that supported you to be kind towards yourself?*
- *Was there a challenge you were able to overcome recently?*
- *Can you remember forgiving yourself for a mistake recently?*

Are there some of these actions you could use to increase your self-kindness?

- *Taking a break when working hard.*
- *Speaking kindly to yourself when upset.*
- *Letting go of blaming yourself when things around you don't go well.*
- *Risking trying out new things.*

Remember: everyone makes mistakes, it's normal, so we are normal as well as special! It can be helpful to focus on what goes well and things we are grateful for.

SELF-REFLECTION WRITING

How Self-compassionate Are You?

These questions are adapted for young people from questions developed from the research by Neff (2003), to help people start to notice their own levels of self-care and self-criticism. They are presented here as part of psychoeducation and rapport-building – both in individual sessions and in group work.

See worksheet on the next page.

Here are some aspects of something important we can explore together: Self-compassion.

Being kind to yourself means:

- *Accepting your thoughts – even if you don't like them – without judgement.*
- *Noticing any criticism of yourself and softening it, even letting it go.*
- *You will have fewer negative feelings about yourself.*
- *You may not have so many upsets with things going on around you.*
- *Not being overwhelmed with negative feelings.*

Take a moment to reflect on each of these questions about how you typically react to yourself. Then jot down a word or two that comes to mind in response. Then we can talk about what the questions mean to you.

- *Are there things you judge yourself for?*
- *What words do you use to yourself after making a mistake, or when you feel embarrassed about yourself?*
- *How did it feel to have a friend accept you, or judge you, when you have made a mistake or said something embarrassing?*
- *What feelings go with being highly critical of yourself?*
- *What do you do when you are being hard on yourself?*
- *What does kindness from others look like to you?*
- *How might you feel if you practised being kind to yourself?*
- *How might you feel if you could accept yourself exactly as you are?*

SELF-REFLECTION WRITING WORKSHEET: How self-compassionate are you?		
	Questions to reflect on:	*Your response in words, phrases or sentences:*
1	*Are there things you judge yourself for?*	
2	*What words do you use to yourself after making a mistake, or when you feel embarrassed about yourself?*	
3.	*How did it feel to have a friend accept you, or judge you, when you have made a mistake or said something embarrassing?*	
4	*What feelings go with being highly critical of yourself?*	
5	*What do you do when you are being hard on yourself?*	
6	*What does kindness from others look like to you?*	
7	*How might you feel if you practised being kind to yourself?*	
8.	*How might you feel if you could accept yourself exactly as you are?*	

MANDALA FREEDOM

Colouring Circles with the Wrong Hand

This activity provides a "warm-up" for participants to gain confidence in spontaneous expression with mandala circles. Prepare three large circles, each on an A3 size sheet of paper, and arrange these on a table with a range of crayons or coloured pencils available.

This activity is a warm-up for using colours and lines to express yourself. We will explore three quick ways of becoming freer in art expression.

Take a tall stretch, a deep breath, give your body a shake and come close to the table with the circles and crayons.

Firstly: Close your eyes, and with your non-dominant hand, the hand you don't normally use for writing, feel where the paper is in front of you and where the crayons are. Without looking, take up a crayon with the hand you normally do not use for writing or drawing.

Take a deep breath and relax it out. Tune in to how you feel right now. When you are ready, simply start drawing patterns or shapes onto the page, without looking. Draw patterns or shapes that seem to go with how you feel when you are upset or angry. Could you do this as quickly as you can? Keep your eyes closed for now. When you are ready, have a look at what you created. Would you like to share how it feels to draw that way, and how your creation looks to you?

Secondly: With open eyes now, look at the crayon colours. Focus on another circle on a fresh page, and when you are ready, with your non-dominant hand, start quickly making some patterns or shapes that seem to go with how you feel when you are having fun on a holiday. Make these in and around the next circle. When you are ready, you might like to share how it feels to draw that way, and how your creation looks to you.

Thirdly: With your eyes open, take up two crayons you like, and with one in each hand, start creating patterns or shapes in the final circle, that seem to go with how you feel at the moment. Try this with both hands at the same time. When you feel ready, you might like to share how it feels to draw that way, and how your creation looks to you.

Was there anything you noticed about expressing yourself in the mandala circles in these three different ways?

MANDALA FREEDOM

Drawing Music

Prepare three large circles, each on an A3 size sheet of paper, and arrange these on a table with a range of crayons or coloured pencils available. Select three music tracks (without lyrics) that express quite different moods: e.g., strong drumming, gentle flowing music, happy playful music and dance rhythms. Tracks can be played for between approximately 1.5 and 2.5 minutes each.

Would you like to stand up and stretch a bit? Take a few deep breaths. Stand at the table, and get ready to listen to some music. This activity uses music to inspire you to express yourself with colours and lines.

For this activity, could you listen carefully, then when you are ready, express your responses in the mandala circles as quickly as you can, with colours, lines, shapes and maybe some pictures.

Play the first track of music.

1. *As you listen, consider:*
   - *Does your body like the music? Or not? Does it seem to say "Yes" or "No"?*
   - *What mood does this music have?*
   - *Is there anywhere inside you where you can feel the music?*
   - *Does the music make you want to move?*
   - *Are there colours that go with this music?*
   - *Is there a shape or some lines or pictures that go with this music?*
2. *Draw quickly now in the circle – use whatever lines, colours, shapes, pictures you feel go with the music.*
3. *See if you would like to add a word or two that goes with the way the music felt.*

Steps 1–3 are repeated with each music track.

- *When You Are Ready, Would You Like To*
- *Show your creations and say something about them?*
- *Are there any tracks you particularly liked or disliked?*
- *Was this activity easy or difficult for you?*
- *Is there one of the drawings you like most?*

SPEED ART

Drawing Feelings

You will need a large sheet of paper, divided into four segments, and a selection of crayons or coloured pencils.

This activity is designed to help you become more confident in expressing yourself through using colours, lines, shapes and pictures. It can be helpful to practice expressing feelings with crayons on paper, as quickly as possible, so there is no time to worry about drawing skills.

When we do it very quickly, there is no time to worry about it, or struggle to get your drawing perfect. We call this "Speed Art". Would you like to try it?

So, you have paper and crayons in front of you. In this warm-up activity, I will invite you to close your eyes just for a moment, take a deep breath and listen to the four brief stories I will describe. When you hear the story, see if you can – as quickly as possible – use the crayons to show how you might feel if you were in this situation. There is no right or wrong way to do this activity. It is like your own experiment.

You might use lines, you might create shapes, there could be just colours, there could be pictures you draw. See if you can make up your own ways to show how you might feel in these situations, in each of the four sections on the page. We will go through the four situations, and then we can talk about how it felt to do the activity.

Situation 1: You have just been told that your best friend is moving away to the other side of the country, and you may not see them again for a while. (pause while they draw)

Situation 2: You have just been told that you and your family have won some money, and there are plans being made for a very exciting holiday. (pause while they draw)

Situation 3: You arrive home one day to find your room has been messed up. You don't know why, you don't know who did it. But it is very messy! (pause while they draw)

Situation 4: You have just completed a relaxation activity. It was an activity you enjoyed, and now you feel calmer than usual. (pause while they draw)

How did it feel to express yourself this way with speed art?

Was there one situation that seemed easiest to show the feelings about?

WRITTEN REFLECTIONS

Sentence Starters

Participants can use the following prompts to support reflection on, and express in writing about, their experience during an activity. The prompts can be offered verbally; however, providing them in written on a page – like a worksheet – and inviting a written response can add depth to their reflection and feeling of freedom and choice in responding.

The review process can support integration of an activity and will be most useful if the participant has experienced any emotional response.

Have a look over (or listen to) these sentence starters and see if there might be a few that seem interesting to respond to.

Notice if any words or statements form in your mind. Then could you add a word or two, or complete the whole sentence?

- *What I liked best was …*
- *The most difficult part was …*
- *I felt good when …*
- *I was upset by …*
- *The strongest feeling was …*
- *One new idea is …*
- *I now want to …*

When you feel finished, look over what you wrote and see if there might be a few things you would like to talk about.

REFLECTION WITH CLAY

My Feelings in Clay

Air-drying clay is recommended for this activity, as it can be kept and hardened for the participant. Having some hand wipes available will be ideal.

This activity helps us get used to expressing ourselves through our hands by shaping clay.

PART A: Exploring qualities of the clay

- *Take hold of your clay, and allow your fingers and hands to begin to explore the clay.*
- *Take a few slow full breaths. Feel free to close your eyes to help focus on your hands.*
- *Take a moment to be quiet and still.*
- *Let your thoughts drift. Allow thoughts, feelings and ideas to float up and then pass by.*
- *Keep your focus returning to the clay in your hands.*
- *When you feel ready, begin to work with the clay, let your hands guide you. What do your hands want to do?*
- *Note how the clay feels in your hand. Can you feel the qualities of the clay, its softness, its resistance, its weight?*
- *Keep feeling the sensations in your hand, the way your hands want to shape the clay.*
- *Note any thoughts that arise as you handle the clay, and see if you can let them go.*
- *Would you like to share anything about how that felt?*

PART B: Expressing feelings

- *In this second stage of the activity, we will focus more on our feelings.*
- *See if you can become aware of your feelings, your mood right now.*
- *Allow the clay to be shaped by your hands, as if you were putting your mood and feelings into the clay. It might help to close your eyes and let your hands do the work.*
- *Take a few deep breaths. Can your feelings flow into the clay? Try not to plan the shapes you are making. How would your hands shape the clay to show those feelings?*
- *When you are ready, place the clay on the table, stand up, walk around and come back to see what you have created.*
- *Is there any way you would like to shape it further?*
- *Would you like to say anything about this second stage of the activity?*
- *As you look at the final shape of the clay, does anything stand out to you?*
- *Is there anything that is familiar or strange about the shape to you?*
- *Could you share a few words that might go with the shape you have created?*

GETTING TO KNOW YOU DISCUSSION

Who Are We?

This discussion activity is ideal for starting group work.

This activity is really a discussion. It is all about getting to know a bit more about what you like and don't like, what things are important to you.

Sit comfortably, take a deep breath, close your eyes for a moment, relax and tune in to your body. See if you can be aware of your body, your mood and your energy right now.

I will ask a question, and see if you could think about it for a moment, see what comes into your mind. Then you are welcome to share your thoughts about the question.

I hope you find the questions interesting. Here we go!

Ask questions and provide time for reflection and discussion, before moving on to the next.

What might be your:

- *Favourite TV show or movie or video game, and are there any you don't like?*
- *Favourite singers, songs, bands or music, and ones you don't like?*
- *Favourite animals and pets?*
- *Best thing about school? What could be better?*
- *Main interests, hobbies, skills?*
- *Family's best fun activity?*
- *Main worries in your life at the moment?*
- *Favourite thing about yourself?*

Could you think of two or three words about how this discussion activity felt to you?

Was there one question that seemed most important to you?

Are there any other topics you would have liked to talk about that we should add to the list?

SOMATIC AWARENESS PRACTICE

What's Happening in My Body?

Participant draws (or is provided with) an A3 size body outline. Have crayons or pencils ready.

This activity is about finding out how your body is feeling at the moment.

See if you could relax on the carpet. See if you would like to close your eyes to help you tune in and focus inside your body. Could you take several slow, full breaths?

Can you take a moment to tune into your body? Check around on the inside, feel what is there. What can you discover? Begin in your head, and move your attention gradually from your head down through your body to your fingers and toes.

See if you can pay attention through your body and look for the different things I mention. If you find the feelings I suggest, draw them on the body outline. Pretend it is a map of you. See if you can tell what colours and what lines could be used to describe what you find.

Then relax again and wait for the next thing to look for. If you do not find anything, just relax and wait for the next search. Sometimes there is one area, sometimes more. It could be a small area, it could be large.

Take time to search for what I mention. It could be found in your head, your shoulders, your arms and hands, your chest, belly, back, hips, legs and feet.

If participants are able to locate a particular sensation, they are invited to choose appropriate colours and express with lines and shading what they have found, on the body outline.

Is there anywhere inside that is …

- *cool or cold*
- *warm or hot?*
- *awake or sleepy?*
- *tight and holding, or relaxed and free?*

Is there anything else you've found inside that hasn't been mentioned?

Would you like to share what you found?

How did it feel for you during the activity?

REFLECTING ON RELAXATION

What Helps You Relax and Play?

It is normal to feel stressed at times. If we notice we are stressed, it can be good to have a plan about how to de-stress, or relax, how to unwind, let go of worries, and be ready to play. I'm going to read a rather long list of ways that can help people relax.

Listen as I read them out. As you listen, you can share:

- *If you do any of these activities,*
- *If you can hear two or three ideas that you have not tried that might help you relax,*
- *Can you think of something you love to do to help you relax that should be added to the list?*

OK, so here is the list:

- *listening to relaxing music*
- *finding a quiet place to hang out*
- *lying down under a blanket or doona*
- *lying on the grass watching the clouds float by with a friend*
- *digging in the garden*
- *playing with pets*
- *playing a musical instrument*
- *colouring in*
- *painting with watercolours*
- *enjoying great snacks*
- *storytelling*
- *swimming on a hot day*
- *watching trees blowing in the wind*
- *story reading*
- *watching a movie*
- *playing board games*
- *chilling out with an iPad*
- *finger painting*
- *sitting by a fire, with a marshmallow on a stick*
- *moulding playdough or clay*
- *sitting on the beach or beside a river*
- *singing – by yourself or with others*

Could you share something about how you feel when you do your favourite relaxing activities?

3 A Fern in the Forest

Visualisation, Relaxation and Stillness Stories for Young People 7–10 Years

This chapter provides child-friendly mindfulness and relaxation activities, and is designed to support young people from approximately 7 to 10 years. The activities/games/stories blend skills in visualisation, use of breath, relaxation, and focusing attention in order to support self-connection, relaxation and well-being. There are recommendations for the integration of activities through artistic expression.

DOI: 10.4324/9781003716501-3

RELAXATION STORY

A Fern in the Forest

This is an activity that calls on your imagination to help you relax. Sometimes it is fun not to be you, to pretend to be something else.

I will tell a story and see if you can listen and imagine what it might look like. And, if you want to, you could do the movements in the story. You will be in the story, but not as you, imagining you are something else!

I'm going to ask you to begin this activity standing up. Can you stand up now? Give your body a stretch, and take a deep breath.

You may like to close your eyes to help you imagine. OK, so see if you could picture yourself as a young fern in a green forest. There is some space around you in this bushland, and it is early in the day.

See in your mind's eye what you – the young fern – looks like. Imagine the space around you and the green bushes, trees and wildflowers. Imagine your shape. Imagine how you would feel if you were a fern in the forest.

And now, imagine the sky is growing darker and cloudy. The wind is blowing.

A storm is moving in! Now the wind is blowing the fern. There is thunder, rain and wind.

Imagine you are the fern, the wind is blowing you and it is blowing all around you. You are very flexible. You bend and sway with the wind. The wind blows you in all directions.

Now rain is falling on the forest. You can feel the drops of rain on your branches. The rain trickles down and soaks into the earth.

Now the weather quietens. The wind dies down. The forest is still and quiet again. Your roots soak up the rain. You feel fresh and strong now.

The sun comes out from behind the clouds. The air is warm again.

You are a young fern, still unfolding, still growing, still uncurling. Could your body show this? Are there any movements?

It is a bright new morning. There are areas of sunshine and areas of shade around you. Imagine the grasses, the trees, the colours and all the shapes of the forest.

Can you hear the birds? And the breeze gently blowing through the leaves, high up in the trees?

This breeze is beginning to make you sway and dance. This gentle breeze keeps changing directions. You are bending. You are flexible. You are alive with gentle movements. Your roots are firm in the earth, and you are swaying free in the breeze.

Could you take a minute to imagine swaying and your branches dancing in the breeze? Could you take a full breath and let your body show this?

(pause)

In this warmth, your fronds, your tender new branches are beginning to unfold. They are spreading out to receive the warmth of the sun. Imagine the energy of the sun flowing into you.

Some little ants are suddenly running up your side! Do they tickle? You can shake them off if you want to.

The breeze has stopped. You become still again. The forest is still. Picture the grass and trees, birds and warmth, and breathe the feeling of all this into you.

Can you become aware of your full size? Feel how tall you are.

See in your mind's eye what you are part of, what is around you, what you are connected with in this forest.

Imagine the water from the rain is rising up from the ground, up through the middle of you, to the tiny leaves at your tips. And your tips feel the warmth of the sun.

What would you look like to someone walking through the forest? What could they see? Could you imagine what you look like to someone walking past?

And, what is the main feeling inside you as this fern? Can you be in touch with that feeling?

See if you could feel that and be still and quiet for a moment now.

When you are ready, come back to being yourself, a person again.

When you are ready, move a little, open your eyes, look about.

Take a moment to be in touch with your feelings from being the fern.

You might like to draw something now.

Maybe you could draw how it felt to be a fern in the forest, or what you would look like – as a fern – to bushwalkers passing by.

Are there any words you could write down that go with how you feel now?

BREATHING GAMES

Balloons and Whales

Taking a few deep breaths can help you relax, feel more peaceful and awake. Here are some short breathing games that use your imagination to help you take some deep breaths.

Before we start the breathing games, lean back and relax, maybe lie down and get comfortable.

Have you noticed what happens in your body when you breathe? Put your hands on your chest. Can you feel your chest move as your breath comes and goes? Notice that movement under your hands.

Take a big breath in and let it out. How does that feel? How much does your chest move when you breathe?

Can you breathe in so much air that your body feels like it is growing huge? OK, now let all the air out.

Now move your hands down to your ribs, feel what's happening with the next two breaths, as you empty all the air out. Now put one hand on your chest and one on your tummy. See if you can continue to feel what is happening in your body as you play the breathing games.

Here are a few ways to breathe to get ready for the breathing games.

First: *Take a breath in through your nose, and let the air out through your mouth. Feel what is happening under your hands when you do that.*

Now: *Take three fast breaths - in and out, very quickly. Feel what is happening under your hands again.*

Next: *Take a big breath in through your right nostril and then let the air out through your left nostril. You can use a finger to help if you like.*

Then, take the next breath in through the left nostril, and out through the right. It is a bit weird, isn't it?

And lastly: *Take a big breath very, very slowly. How slowly could you breathe in?*

And then when you are full of air, let go, let the air out.

Let's try that once more:

Take a big breath very, very slowly. How slowly could you breathe in? And then when you are full of air, let go, let the air out.

So, now we are ready for the breathing games.

1. ***The first breathing game uses imaginary balloons***

   Actually, for this game I'm going to suggest you pretend you are a balloon. Imagine someone is blowing you up. They use six slow, big, full breaths to blow you up.

   OK, so make yourself into this huge balloon. And you take in a breath with each number I count. Here we go: 1- breathe in, 2- breathe in, 3, 4, 5, and 6. So you are full now. Now someone let the balloon go. Imagine you fly around the room making a funny noise as you let your breath out. Can you make the balloon noise?

OK, let's try again. You are a balloon. Someone is blowing you up. Take in a breath with each number I count. Here we go: 1- breathe in, 2- breathe in a bit more, 3, 4, 5, and 6. Now let the balloon go. You fly around the room making a funny noise as you let your breathe out.

And you rest.

2. ***The second breathing game is called "the whale"***

Imagine you are a large beautiful whale swimming through the ocean. You have been down deep, under the water. You move gracefully through the cool water, going down deep, then rising up to the surface to breathe.

Now you are pushing up to the surface from deep below. You have been holding your breath for a long time. As your head rises above the waves, you breathe out, quickly and powerfully. Try that. Imagine a fine spray of water bursting out as the breath releases.

Then, very quickly you take a deep breath in, hold it, and imagine diving down deep again. And then you come back to the surface. Let the old air out and take in a fresh breath. Imagine diving deep, swirling through the water, and now leaping up, and taking another breath.

And rest.

3. ***And here's one more breathing game. It is game is about a fire-breathing dragon***

Imagine you are a giant fire-breathing dragon. Could you stand tall and strong and imagine you are this dragon?

You take in giant dragon breaths. Then you can send your breath out with flames! The long red and yellow flames show your friends how strong you are.

I wonder how far you could send those flames? Let's try. Take in a deep, deep breath. Imagine lighting up your flames. Breathe out and send the flames across the room. That's great!

Take another breath – in, in, in – and send some flames out again. See if you can send the fire even further this time. That is great.

Now let yourself have a moment to rest. Relax and tune in, and check how you feel inside now.

If you feel like it, you might like to rest a bit longer, or draw something that shows how you feel inside after those breathing games.

VISUALISATION STORY

An Iceberg Melts

This is a short story about a large iceberg that floats away from the frozen South Pole, into warm waters. And it slowly melts. You may have seen pictures of icebergs. An iceberg is a huge chunk of frozen water, sometimes as big as a city building, floating in the ocean. It is usually very big, with just its tip rising above the water. Most of the iceberg is out of sight, under the water.

For this story, I will invite you to imagine you are the iceberg.

So, lean back in a comfortable chair, or lie on a soft floor with some cushions. Find a comfortable place, and relax as much as you can. You can close your eyes if you like, to help you concentrate. Take three big slow breaths, and relax the out-breath.

Are you ready?

So, imagine yourself as an iceberg floating in the icy ocean near the South Pole. It is very white and very cold there. Imagine you are the iceberg now.

You are slowly moved through the icy waters by the wind and the water currents.

You are floating away from the cold, towards the warmer countries. You are heading towards the warmth.

Where the sun touches you, you start to soften, to melt a little.

You are heading north towards the warm places. In the warmer countries, there are palm trees and beautiful beaches, and the sun shines very hot.

The sun shines down now on you, on that part of you that is above the water. And you want to be warm. You want to move towards the warm places.

And the ocean around you is warming up. So, there is warmth above you and warmth below.

You know what happens when ice warms up – it melts. So, how would that feel to the iceberg as it starts to melt? What does it feel like to warm up and melt into the ocean, to be part of the ocean? Could you imagine your body is slowly melting? This means that your muscles are relaxing, and tension and worry are melting away.

Instead of being cold and hard, you can flow with the warm ocean currents, becoming warm, and visit beaches all around the world.

Imagine yourself melting now. Imagine that the water inside you, which was frozen, is becoming warm and blending in with the whole ocean.

The sun is hot, the air is warm and the water is warm. Imagine yourself being part of the ocean, flowing with the warm ocean current. (pause)

Imagine the hard ice becomes soft, then slushy, and melts into the water. Are there any frozen parts left? Has all the ice inside you melted away? Could your body relax even more?

Are your arms warm and melted yet?

Tune in to your legs, are they warm and melted?

How does it feel in the middle of your body? Can you imagine the middle of your body becoming warm, melting and floating with the ocean current?

Imagine all of you is warm and melted now, floating gently with the ocean, towards the warm beaches.

You are part of the great oceans. There are fish swimming through you. You flow into waves that rise and fall. You are part of the warm waters, flowing, gently moving. You have arrived at the warm places.

(pause)

Now take a slow full breath, move a little, move your toes, move your fingers. When you are ready, let your eyes open. When you are ready, come back to being you, here in this room.

Can you think of any times when it would be useful to feel soft and melted like this?

Would you like to draw something that reminds you of how it felt to go from frozen to warm and melted and soft?

ACTIVE RELAXATION

Moving in Slow Motion

This activity aims to enhance body awareness and lead to muscles relaxing. Keeping the movements at a very, very slow speed brings awareness to come into the limbs. This has a quietening effect on thoughts, feelings and muscle tone. Some quiet flowing music may support the process.

Ideally participants lie on a carpeted floor on their backs, with limbs spread out.

Give your body a moment to relax a little, and settle down onto the carpet. You may like to close your eyes to help you focus inside yourself. Take a few deep breaths and relax as much as you can.

Leaving your arms resting on the carpet, begin turning your wrists very, very slowly – so slowly that the movement is between the point of stillness and movement. There is nothing now to think about, but this slow movement, feel the little changes in the muscles as you turn your wrists.

Now focus on and start to slowly move your ankles. They can turn in the same direction, or opposite, it doesn't matter, don't think about it, just feel the slow movement.

Next, focus on your head, turning it slowly. The movement is so slow. You might notice you want to speed up, but for this activity, the best thing is slowness.

The next step is a bit more complicated. Could you slowly move an ankle and a wrist from opposite sides of the body? Try this for a moment. Now change to the opposite wrist and ankle.

I wonder if it is possible to add your head to the parts that are moving now? See if you can keep your head, ankle and wrist moving together very slowly.

Now slowly, gently kneel up, take another deep breath and let the upper part of your body turn from one side to the other very slowly through space. Try that for a while, see how it feels, keep focusing on the small movements inside your body as you turn

Next, slowly stand up, see if you can turn your whole body through space, let it flow from one side to the other. Is it possible to let go of control, surrender to the flowing? Just let everything move, flow, turn.

And now it is time to be still. Feel the stillness. Is it really stillness? Bring your focus inside yourself now. What do you notice? How would you describe it? (pause.)

As you focus inside, see if you could move to the paper with a circle on it and the crayons and see if you could describe what you noticed inside with colours and lines.

THE LAZY RELAXATION

You Don't Have to Do Anything

I call this a lazy activity because you don't have to do anything. This activity actually happens in your imagination. So, I'm not sure it really is an activity! It uses the power of your mind to help your body become calm and relaxed.

For this activity, it might be best to lie on your back, on a soft carpet with a cushion under your head.

In this activity you do not have to do anything! You are just asked to imagine, to pretend your body is relaxing. When you imagine relaxing, your body might begin to let go of worries – all by itself.

Move your knees up with your feet flat on the carpet, in a balanced position – so your knees are just happy holding themselves up. Your arms are by your side, with your hands resting on each side of your tummy.

So, let's begin the lazy relaxation.

Imagine your neck is soft and floppy. Think of it as if your neck is growing a little longer. Imagine that.

Tune in to the middle of your body, let it relax. Imagine the middle of your body is growing a little longer and wider, and settling down onto the floor. Could you picture this happening? Could you let a picture of this relaxing come into your mind?

Next, tune in to your chest. Tell your chest it can let go, it can melt down, it can relax a bit. Imagine your chest is relaxing, just like melted cheese on a warm pizza.

Now, imagine your shoulders settling down. Let your shoulders relax and spread out. Allow your body to do this if it wants to.

Your arms and hands are used to doing things. Now imagine they are still and a bit heavy. Imagine your hands are like two puppies that have been playing all day, and they are now still and quiet, deep in sleep.

Tune into your belly next. Imagine your belly is letting go of the worries of life. Imagine your tummy is resting, it is like a kitten curled up by a warm fire.

Imagine your legs letting go of all the walking, running, and kicking and climbing. Then imagine your legs becoming calm like a lake, with no waves, no boats, no breeze.

It is quite likely that you will find your body wanting to take a few full breaths as you follow this activity, so encourage these breaths, but don't try to DO it.

So, let's go through the body again. Tune in to your chest. Imagine your chest, your lungs are letting go, melting down, relaxing.

Imagine your shoulders relaxing and spreading out from each other a little, settling down onto the carpet.

Now imagine your hands and arms are relaxed and a bit heavy.

Tune into your belly now. Is anything tight in there? Imagine your belly is letting go of all the worries.

Imagine your legs are letting go of all the rushing about. And imagine your legs becoming calm and still.

Let your whole body take a full breath, and relax.

Tune in to your knees, imagine they are floating up towards the ceiling a little bit. Picture your knees as clouds for a moment, floating, relaxed and soft.

Check through inside, from head to toes. Imagine all your worries melting away now, like snow melting on a hot afternoon, turning into water and flowing away.

Let's go through the body one more time, starting with your head and neck.

And, tune in again to your chest. Imagine this area letting go, melting down, relaxing.

Imagine your shoulders relaxing and spreading out from each other a little, becoming wider.

Now imagine your hands and arms are relaxed and a bit heavy.

And tune into your belly now. Is anything tight? Imagine your belly is letting go of worries.

Imagine your legs letting go of all the rushing about. Then imagine your legs becoming calm and still.

Let your body take in a full breath, and relax it out.

Imagine your knees floating up towards the ceiling a little. Picture them again as clouds for a moment.

And checking through inside, letting all parts of you be soft and relaxed now.

Could you imagine all your worries melting and flowing away?

Stay like this for a moment. And see what you can notice inside you right now.

It is time to finish this activity. Slowly move your toes a little and stretch your fingers.

When you are ready, turn onto your side, maybe curl up for a moment. Then, when you are ready, gently sit up.

Would you like to draw something to show how you feel now? Or tell someone about your experience with the lazy relaxation?

VISUALISING BEAUTY

My Favourite Place in Nature

This is a relaxation activity that you could remember and use later if there are times when you feel stressed or worried. It could help you feel calm and happy, and it might be helpful at bedtime.

Get comfortable. Relax and tune in to how you feel now. Take in a deep breath and relax it out.

See if you can remember a beautiful, safe place in nature. This will be a place which attracts you, a place you love to be, a place with some beauty, where you feel safe and happy, a place where worries can be left behind.

This place could be a favourite beach, or in the mountains, by a river or in a park. It may be a place where you can see the sky, trees, flowers, and maybe some beautiful views. It could be a special part of your garden at home or at your grandparents' place.

Can you choose one beautiful favourite place you know, and remember it now.

Could you take another deep breath and imagine being back at this beautiful place in nature?

See if you could imagine moving through this beautiful place. Be interested in what you remember, what you see. Is there anyone there with you?

Take time and allow the pictures of this favourite place to soak in, and enjoy them. (pause)

What stands out for you? What would you notice most in this place?

What are the main things you would see? Imagine looking up and down, from side to side. Let the pictures of this place come into your mind.

What would you hear in this place? What would you smell? What would you like to touch?

What would be the main feelings in you when you are there?

If the feeling of this beautiful place in nature could live inside you somewhere, where would that be?

Take a moment to see if this feeling would be in your head? your chest?

your tummy, or your arms or legs?

Imagine the beauty of this place is inside you now.

When you want to, you could imagine coming back to this beautiful place, and see if you can find the feeling of it inside you, again.

When you are ready, say "goodbye" to this place, and come back to the room you are in now.

So remember, in your imagination, you can visit this beautiful place whenever you want to.

Right now, would you like to do a quick sketch to remind you of the main parts of that beautiful place? It could be a picture of the whole place, or just a part of it.

It does not matter if you are good at drawing or not. Just quickly sketch something that will remind you of it.

If it helps, you could write down a few of your memories, or just a few words, about this place in nature.

You might like to give your sketch a title.

You may like to put the sketch up somewhere you can see it each day, and it can remind you of this beautiful, peaceful place in nature.

VISUALISING PEACE

The Peaceful Park

This peaceful story could help you feel calm. It might be useful if you have trouble going to sleep at night. See if you can imagine yourself in the story.

I have the words. You can make up the pictures in your mind.

The pictures that go with the stories will come out of your imagination and show themselves inside, if you watch closely inside. I hope that listening to the story and imagining the pictures will help you relax and feel restful.

It would be good to lie down or rest in a comfy chair. Sometimes closing your eyes helps you listen to the story and imagine the pictures more clearly.

You can watch the pictures that bubble up into your mind, as if you were an artist preparing to make a storybook. You could also imagine that you are in the story, and the story is about you.

Ready? Imagine you are in a beautiful park on a fine, warm afternoon. It is a large park, with plenty of space for everyone.

Your friends and family are playing nearby, but you have wandered off a little and are by yourself in a quiet part of the park.

You are lying on your back on the warm, soft grass, looking up at the blue sky.

There are tall trees and green bushes around you, and lots of bright flowers. Birds are flying about and singing in the trees.

You have been watching the trees moving in the breeze, swaying from side to side. You see the branches bend and dance, as the leaves flutter, way up above you. Sometimes you wish you could be riding up there on those branches, free like a bird, swaying on the breeze.

Behind the trees, you see blue sky and white clouds. And now you watch the clouds drift by. As they float across the sky, they change shape. Watch the clouds now.

What shapes are they making? And do the shapes remind you of anything?

Now you listen to the birds. They are singing to each other, but now they have noticed you. They are looking at you. They are above you now, can you see? They are singing just for you.

What do you think the birds would say if they could sing to you in human language?

Now the birds fly off, called away by their families. You are resting warm and comfortable on the grass. And soon it will be time to go back to your friends.

You close your eyes for a moment. You can feel the warm air on your skin and deep inside you feel your heart beating. You rest here for a while, enjoying the warmth.

When you feel ready, you might like to come back into this room and have a stretch. Open your eyes, and look around.

Would you like to draw something from the story that can help you remember feeling peaceful?

VISUALISATION FOR SLEEP

The Full Moon

This peaceful story could help you feel calm. It might be useful if you have trouble going to sleep at night. See if you can imagine yourself in the story.

I have the words. You can make up the pictures in your mind.

The pictures that go with the stories will come out of your imagination and show themselves inside, if you watch closely inside. I hope that listening to the story and imagining the pictures will help you relax and feel restful.

It would be good to lie down or rest in a comfy chair. Sometimes closing your eyes helps you listen to the story and imagine the pictures more clearly.

You can watch the pictures that bubble up into your mind, as if you were an artist preparing to make a storybook. You could also imagine that you are in the story, and the story is about you.

Ready? In this story, you are enjoying nature again. This time, imagine you are on a camping trip, you and your best friends are in the bush.

It is past your usual bedtime, but you are not tired. There is a bright full moon, reflecting a silver and white light over the bush around you.

Your friends are nearby, but they are not talking.

You have just cooked a meal together on your campfire. You ate the meal and talked and joked for a while, and now you are lying on your sleeping bag, watching the night.

It is warm and peaceful.

The flames of the fire leap up and down. Yellow and orange shapes light up the darkness. Watch in your mind's eye the colours – the yellow and orange and red flames.

You watch the flames for a while. In the flames, tiny flame creatures appear and disappear – and float up into the sky.

You look up. The moon is round and seems to be glowing. You can just make out the shadows of the mountains of the moon. These shapes look almost like a face, smiling down at you.

There are no clouds in the sky. You can see millions of planets and stars. As you watch the stars, you imagine joining them up, drawing lines from one to another, until they make huge pictures above you.

As you listen you can hear insects singing.

They seem to be glad of the darkness as they call to each other.

Your sleeping bag is soft and comfortable. The insects sing a sleepy song. The air is warm. You relax and rest.

When you feel ready, you might like to come back into this room and have a stretch. Open your eyes, and look around.

Would you like to draw something from the story that can help you remember feeling peaceful?

VISUALISATION FOR REST

The Mountain Stream

This peaceful story could help you feel calm. It might be useful if you have trouble going to sleep at night. See if you can imagine yourself in the story.

I have the words. You can make up the pictures in your mind.

The pictures that go with the stories will come out of your imagination and show themselves inside, if you watch closely inside. I hope that listening to the story and imagining the pictures will help you relax and feel restful.

It would be good to lie down or rest in a comfy chair. Sometimes closing your eyes helps you listen to the story and imagine the pictures more clearly.

You can watch the pictures that bubble up into your mind, as if you were an artist preparing to make a storybook. You could also imagine that you are in the story, and the story is about you.

Ready? It's a fresh spring morning. You have slept well. After breakfast, you pack up and go for a walk in the bush.

You are walking a little behind your friends, enjoying yourself and looking all around you.

You are wearing your very old sneakers as you walk up along a stream, splashing over the smooth stones of the shallow parts of the water. You move in and out of the sun under the shadows of the trees that line the stream.

You look about at the old trees. Some have been knocked over by floods. Some are new and young and straight. There are many shades of green in the leaves and in the grass around you.

As you stroll along, you can hear the sound of the water flowing over the stones.

Listen to the sound of the water. It is like a gentle song. The water is calling to you, encouraging you.

Your friends sit down to rest, a bit further up the stream.

And you sit for a while on a smooth, warm rock at the water's edge.

Beside you, you notice two small lizards warming themselves in the sun. They are almost the same colour as the rock. They are staying very still.

You take off your sneakers and dip your feet in the cool, flowing stream.

Now you lie back on the warm rock. The sound of the water flowing over the rocks fills your ears. And you listen.

The water sounds are singing, speaking; they could be telling you something.

Take a few deep breaths of the fresh air and relax. Your friends are resting, so you can also relax here for a while.

When you feel ready, you might like to come back into this room and have a stretch. Open your eyes, and look around.

Would you like to draw something from the story that can help you remember feeling peaceful?

4 Imaginary Journeys

Visualisation, Role-Play and Movement Adventures for Relaxation and Resilience for Young People 7–10 Years

This chapter is designed to support young people from approximately 7 to 10 years. The activities/games/stories blend skills in somatic awareness, controlled movement, relaxation, visualisation, emotional expression, playfulness and focused attention in order to support ability with relaxation, enhanced self-esteem and resilience.

DOI: 10.4324/9781003716501-4

DE-STRESSING AND ENERGISING

A Star in the Midnight Sky

As the name of this activity suggests, you will be invited to imagine yourself as a star in the sky at night. Before we start this activity, can you stand up, stretch, then tighten all your muscles – as tight as you can. Then let your whole body go floppy. This might help you feel more ready to focus on the story.

Start with your hands and arms, tighten them up for a moment, now add your feet and legs, good, now add your face and then the middle of your body. Hold for a moment – everything tight. Now let go. Go floppy. Let's do that again.

Tighten your hands and arms, hold them tight for a moment, now add your feet and legs, good, now add your face and then the middle of your body. Hold everything tight for a moment. Now let go. Go floppy.

Great, now stretch out on your back on the carpet, and let your body be still for a moment.

We will use tensing of muscles and letting them relax in this activity. And you can do this at other times, whenever you feel stressed.

Would you like to be able to float through the sky at night? Would you like to shine like a bright star in the midnight sky?

Can you imagine being a star, one of those stars with five points? Your head is a point of the star, and each arm and leg is one of the other points of the star.

So, think of yourself as a star in the night sky. Stretch out your arms and legs into a star shape. Then relax. Tune in to see how you feel inside right now.

So, you are imagining yourself now as a five-pointed star in the night sky? Your hands and feet and your head are the points of the star. You are floating and shining in a clear night sky.

And, now the star is going to try some exercises. These are exercises that help the star twinkle and shine brighter.

First, pay attention to your right hand. Tighten your right hand, tighten your fingers, close your hand tightly. Then wake up the muscles in the whole of your right arm, from your wrist all the way up to your shoulder. Hold your arm tight for a moment, without lifting it off the carpet. Now let it go, let your whole arm go floppy! Let that point of the star relax.

The next point of the star to focus on is your right foot. Can you tighten your foot and toes? Then tighten your whole right leg, from your ankle right up to your hip. Hold the muscles in your right leg tight for a moment, now let go.

Next, tune in to your left foot. Can you tighten it? See if you can crunch up your toes a bit. Now see if you can tense the muscles all along your left leg, all the way up to your knee, and then up to your hip. Hold this tightness for just a moment, then let go. Be floppy again.

Now focus on the next point of the star, your left hand. Tighten your fingers, let your hand close tight. Then include your whole left arm up to the elbow and up to the shoulder. Tighten it all, hold for a moment and let it go.

Let's go around those points of the star again, helping the star shine bright. Starting with your right hand. Tighten your right hand, tighten your fingers, close your hand tightly. Then hold your arm tight for a moment, without lifting it off the carpet. And, let go!

Now focus on your right foot. Tighten your foot and toes. Then tighten your whole leg, all the way up to the hip. Hold tight for a moment, now let it go.

Next, tighten your left foot. Now tense the muscles all the way along your left leg, all the way up to your hip. Hold this tight for a moment, then let go. And be floppy again.

Now focus on your left hand. Tighten your fingers, let your hand close tight. Then tighten your whole left arm up to the shoulder. Tighten it all, hold for a moment and now let go.

The last point of the star to focus on is your head. See if you can scrunch up your face a bit, squeeze your mouth and eyes shut for a moment. Now hold that tight and also tighten up the middle of your body, tense up your chest and belly, hold tight for a moment, and let go. Let everything be still and soft for a moment.

Let's see if we can do all of that again – the hands, the feet and the head and middle of your body – a little bit faster this time.

So, your right hand: tighten your hand. Tighten your arm – and let go!

Tense your right foot. Tighten your whole leg, hold it tight for a moment – and now relax.

Tighten your left foot. Now tense all along your leg. Hold tight – and relax.

Now tense your left hand. Let your hand close tight. Tighten your whole left arm. Hold for a moment – and let go.

Tense up your face. Now hold that and tighten up the middle of your body, hold tight for a moment – and let go. Let everything be still and soft for a moment.

And, one more time, let's see if we can do all of that again – the hands, the feet and the head and middle of your body – a little bit faster this time.

So, focus on your Right hand. Tighten your hand. Tighten your arm – and let go!

Tense your right foot, your whole leg, hold tight for a moment – and relax.

Tighten your left foot. Now tense all along your leg. Hold tight – and relax.

Now tense your left hand. Let your hand close tight. Tighten your whole left arm. Hold for a moment – and let go.

Tense up your face. Now hold that and tighten up the middle of your body, your chest and belly, hold tight for a moment – and now let go. Let everything be still and soft for a moment.

Now the star can rest. Can you take a moment to feel what's happening inside you at now? Be as still as you can.

Can you feel inside? What do you notice? How does your body feel inside?

You can be as still as you like for a while.

Soon, when you feel ready, you might like to draw something – some colours and lines or shapes, or perhaps a picture – that goes with how the star feels right now after its exercises.

VISUALISING PEACE

You Are the Sunset

This activity is not really an activity, because it happens in your mind. Sometimes helping your mind relax can bring a happy mood and a peaceful feeling to your whole body.

Find a comfortable place to lie down, let your body stretch out, and then relax. Take in a few deep breaths, and let the air flow out by itself.

You can close your eyes for this activity to help your imagination work. See if you can imagine the scene I will describe, and imagine you are in the scene.

Could you begin by imagining it is the end of the day? You are the sunset – the most beautiful sunset ever. The sun is going down, and making wonderful colours in the sky. See the sunset in your mind and imagine you are the sunset.

(pause)

Imagine you are the evening colours across the sky. Some sunsets have lots of orange, pink and red colours. Some have purples and yellows. Some are bright, some have gentle colours. Some have clouds which seem to glow golden.

Can you imagine what colours you would be if you were the sunset? (pause)

Now the sun has disappeared behind the hills. So, you – the sunset – are the colours in the clouds and across the sky.

You are the sunset. You stretch over the rooftops, over the trees, over the hills. You stretch wide across the sky. All around the country, people look up and enjoy your colours, and they start to relax and feel peaceful.

It is the last light of the day. The sky slowly grows darker. Around you, birds are becoming quiet, children go inside for dinner, the humans settle down and the world becomes still.

You are the colours, the sky, the view. You are spread over the distance, stretching wide.

Could you be the sunset for a while? See if you can be still and quiet and imagine your colours.

(pause)

What is the main feeling of the sunset now? What are the main colours and shapes that go with the feeling of being a sunset?

Are there any words for the feeling of being a sunset?

(pause)

Take another deep breath and slowly come back to being yourself. Move a little and look around you.

When you are ready, if you would like, you could spend some time sketching your shapes and colours as the sunset. You can add some words about how the sunset felt at the end of the day.

You could also talk about any times in your life when it might be helpful to remember being the sunset.

MOVEMENT ROLE-PLAY GAME

A Seal on a Warm Rock

This activity invites you to move at first. It uses your imagination to help you go from action to being more quiet and relaxed. In this activity, you can magically change into anything in each part of the story.

Let's begin with a short warm-up. Take a moment to walk around the room, let your arms swing as you walk, and take in a few deep breaths.

OK, now stop, and just stand still.

Focus on your face for a moment: Imagine the worst foods ever; whatever for you is the worst, the most disgusting, the most foul-tasting. And you have to eat it all! Lots of it!

How would your face show that? What shape would you make with your mouth?

What sounds would you make? Are there any words you would speak?

And now that food has gone. Now imagine your arms are the wind – and it's a very windy day. Make sure you have space around you to swing your arms safely. Your arms are the wild winds, they twirl around and around, faster and faster.

The wind blows and blows, around and around. The wind makes a great noise as it rushes through the trees. Everyone can hear the wind and see its power. Could you make the sound of the wind?

And, now the wind dies down. You can let your arms rest.

Now you can find a comfortable space and lie down on your back.

Stretch your legs up in the air, and use your arms to support your hips. As if your toes were trying to touch the ceiling.

Imagine you are juggling a large soccer ball from foot to foot. Can you imagine the ball? Imagine kicking it gently from foot to foot. Let your legs do the movement.

Now, using both feet, you try to kick the ball up to the roof a few times. See if you can imagine bouncing it off the roof. Now see if you can kick the ball through the ceiling, through the roof, all the way to the moon! Great, and try again!

And let your body relax.

Now, you are part of the ocean, and a big storm is blowing in.

Let yourself move like the ocean – you are the wild waves rising and crashing. There's lots of noise in the storm. Could you make the movements? You could make the sounds. There is lightning and rain. The waves are huge; they rush forward and flow back, over and over.

And then suddenly the storm passes. The ocean settles. The sun comes out. Now it is time to rest on a smooth, warm rock beside the calm ocean.

Imagine now you are a beautiful shiny seal, sunning yourself on the rocks.

When you feel too hot, you slide back into the water and float about. In the water, you dive and turn and twist and float, then slip back up on the rocks to rest.

The ocean is calm, the rocks are smooth and warm, the sun shines. Your friends are nearby. You like to scratch your back and wriggle around, then rest. You are a happy seal on a warm rock. You've had a good lunch and now it's time to rest. Now you are a sleepy seal.

You settle onto the warm rock, and soon you are asleep, with deep, slow breaths.

Maybe you are dreaming of the fun you will have diving and leaping. But for now, you are still.

(pause)

When you are ready, could you sit up? Would you like to draw something to show how you feel after being the seal on the warm rock? Are there any words you could add that go with how you feel? Is there something that might remind you of being the seal?

MOVEMENT ROLE-PLAY GAME

A Twister Unwinds

Here is a story, an imaginary journey, for you to act out. It can help you move, stretch and play, and then become more quiet and peaceful.

As I tell the story see how much you can imagine being the things in the story, and moving like them. See if you can make the sounds and the actions.

You can begin by standing up, stretching your body and taking a few deep breaths.

Make sure you have some space around you.

So, you are a mighty wind, a wind that blows around in circles. You are a cyclone or a twister. You blow around and around in circles, moving across the countryside.

You swirl around on yourself, collecting up everything in the countryside around you.

Show this with your arms. And can you make a large, loud swooshing noise? People are running away from you. You are very strong, full of energy. You spin and spin. You gather up cars, animals, even pull up trees. You spin and spin. You are very powerful.

(pause.)

And, then the weather changes, the twister slows down and becomes a breeze. The twister has faded away, you put down the things you have collected. The twister turns into a very gentle breeze. Could you show the gentle movement of the breeze? It is very light, gentle, almost tickling. Soon it is still.

Let yourself relax now. Flop down on some cushions or in a comfortable chair.

Let yourself be still and quiet. After this storm, it is quiet.

When you are ready to finish, you might like to draw something to remind you of something that you liked best, and how it felt to play it out.

MOVEMENT ROLE-PLAY GAME

The Exploding Volcano

This story could help you move and play, and then become more quiet and peaceful. It is a story for you to act out.

As I tell the story, see how much you can imagine being everything in the story. See if you can make the sounds and the actions of everything in the story.

Make sure you have some space around you. You can begin by standing up, stretching your body, running quickly on the spot for a moment and taking a few deep breaths. Now, listen to what comes next:

This is a simple story; it is about a volcano. Picture yourself as an active volcano. This volcano is a mountain with hot lava, very hot melted rock, deep inside. There is a lot of smoke and steam rising up out of the top of you, into a cloud in the sky. Lava is rock deep under the ground, that is so hot it has turned bright red and melted, and can flow slowly, like super-hot melted chocolate.

From deep down below inside, there is pressure building up from the molten rock, the lava. This lava is pushing up; it wants to escape. It is pushing up against a plug of solid rock at the top. The pressure is growing inside as the lava is pushing up. I think there could be an explosion soon.

Take a position that helps you feel a bit like the volcano, about to explode.

Act out the pressure inside the volcano, show this with your hands, and with all your muscles.

You are the lava pushing up, and pushing up.

Suddenly the plug in the top breaks loose and the lava shoots up with lots of colours and sounds, and smoke and steam. The lava is bright and hot and flares up in all directions. Clouds of smoke and steam fill the sky.

Now you are the orange and red lava, you are flowing down the side of the volcano.

As this liquid rock cools, it begins to flow more slowly. Your movement becomes slow. As the air cools, the rock stops moving and becomes still. And soon it is as still as stone.

Be still like solid stone for a moment. Feel yourself breathing after the eruption. The volcano is peaceful again. The pressure has gone.

When you are ready to finish, you might like to draw something to remind you of what you liked best and how it felt to play it out.

You might like to think about – and talk about – any times when you have felt a bit like a volcano, and what happened then.

MOVEMENT ROLE-PLAY GAME

A Playful Cheetah in the Long Grass

Here is another story for you to act out. It can help you move and play, and then become more quiet and peaceful.

As I tell this story, see how much you can imagine being the animal in it, and moving like the animal. See if you can make the animal's sounds and the actions.

Make sure you have some space around you. You can begin by standing up, stretching your body and taking a few deep breaths.

In this imaginary journey, we go to Africa. We are near the jungle, in the grasslands – wide open spaces covered with tall, thick grasses. There is a cheetah striding through the long grass. A cheetah is like a leopard or lion – it is thin, graceful and very, very fast. It is the fastest of all land animals. Now you are a handsome cheetah, walking proudly through the tall grasses. Imagine that.

Feel all those powerful muscles in your legs as you walk along. Suddenly you see your friend ahead. You feel like playing. You begin to sneak up on your friend. You push through the long grass very slowly now, very quietly.

You plan to pounce on your friend and surprise them. Without being seen, you move carefully and slowly into a good pouncing position. Now you tense every muscle in your body, getting ready to spring out of the long grass.

You take in a deep breath and hold still for a moment. Your friend comes close. They have not seen you. And now you pounce! You leap out to surprise them. You roll about with your friend and have a great game.

Then you have a race. Who will be the fastest? You run up and down until you are tired. Then you lie down and rest together in the shade of a tree. You feel a bit lazy now and rest. Is your heart still beating faster after the leaping and running?

When you are ready, you might like to draw something to remind you of what you liked best about being a cheetah, and how it felt to move like a cheetah.

Are there any words for the power of the cheetah? Are there times when it would be helpful to be like a cheetah?

MOVEMENT ROLE-PLAY GAME

A Colourful Snake beside the Creek

Some people like snakes and think they are very beautiful. Some are afraid of snakes and would like to keep far away from them. Have you seen a real live snake? How did you feel about that, or how would you feel if you saw one?

For this imaginary journey, we go to the bush, beside a creek, to become a python, a young, very beautiful snake with patterns across its back. As I tell the story, see how much you can imagine being the snake, and moving like it. See if you can make the snake movements.

Make sure you have some space around you. You can begin by standing up, stretching your body and taking a few deep breaths. Then settle onto the carpet.

You are a beautiful young snake with colourful patterns along your back. You are curled up on the warm mud beside the creek. You have had a good lunch and you are enjoying the warmth. Your body is very relaxed as you curl around yourself, into a circle.

Suddenly the shadow of an eagle – your worst enemy – passes over you. You slide away very quickly to hide under some rocks.

You are breathing quickly now after your fright. After a while, it is safe to come out. The eagle has passed.

You slide cautiously back to the warm mud beside the creek, but you stay close to the rocks. The clouds have moved away, and the sun is quite hot now.

You decide to go for a swim to cool down. You slip down to the water. Your graceful movements make little waves through the water; you curve through the cool water. And then return to your favourite muddy spot. But you are not comfortable. Your skin feels too tight.

Now you realise that your old skin is tight. You have grown! Snakes like to shed their old skin because it does not stretch as they grow. You get busy twisting yourself about the rocks to help peel off the old skin.

Gradually each part of you wriggles across the rock to pull off the old, dead skin. Feel it coming off, from your head all the way down to your tail. Your new skin is soft and not too tight, the bright colours shine in the sunlight.

(pause)

Now you are free of the tightness. Your body can relax and you can feel free.

You are safe now. The eagle has gone, you are cooled from your swim, and your old tight skin has peeled off. You settle back to rest on the mud. You are breathing fully and resting. Soon you fall asleep.

When you are ready, you might like to draw something to remind you of being the snake and how it felt in each part of the story.

STRENGTH VISUALISATION

The Mysterious Island

This story takes you on an imaginary journey to find a surprise on a mysterious island across the ocean.

You could stand up and do some of the actions in the adventure, or if you like, settle into a comfortable chair and let your mind do all the work.

Imagine you and your tribe live beside the ocean. Imagine that this adventure takes place long, long ago. You live beside the ocean in simple huts, with your family and friends. It is a simple life: you go food gathering, fishing, swimming and playing. This is a time, hundreds and hundreds of years ago, before schools were invented. And life is very simple.

It is a warm, calm night. It is a full moon night. This is the evening that your tribe has gathered to celebrate beside the ocean. You have all worked together to build a huge fire, and there are plans for feasting and drumming and dancing.

So, now you have all had a great feast. You are dancing around the fire with your tribe, some are drumming, some are singing. You dance on into the night. The drums are beating so loudly. Your dancing shadow moves along the sand. It is time for fun.

After the sun sets, the full moon rises high in the sky, lighting up the beach and the ocean. The moon is shining a silver path out across the water. The water is calm, with gentle rhythmic waves.

The night is warm. The drums give you strength. You feel good and strong. As you watch the silver trail of moonlight, you think you see a flash of light out across the ocean. It seems to come from where the sky meets the water. You have a great idea! You want to take your canoe and set out on an adventure across the ocean, to see what caused that flash of light.

See if you can imagine your canoe, a small boat for paddling over the water? You are comfortable in the canoe. You have used it for fishing many times.

It is time to launch the canoe, to slide it down the beach, across the sand, into the water, and you set out over the gentle waves. You have a paddle to push your boat through the water.

You paddle out, following the moon's path. You paddle and paddle, but you don't get tired. You can hear your tribe a long way off in the distance. You can hear water lap against your canoe as you push through the water.

You have paddled so long, aiming for the spot where you thought you saw a light. You notice the daylight starting to glow orange and yellow on the far horizon. And, ahead, you can just see the shape of a mysterious island in the distance.

You have never seen this island before. You know that it is where you are meant to go.

And so you paddle faster now!

You paddle ashore to the island, over the waves. You pull the canoe up the beach. You walk up the sand to the grass. There is no sign of the light. There is a thick jungle in the middle of the island.

You look about and you can see a track through the jungle. You head towards the middle of the island through the trees, through the thick jungle. The track guides you. The track leads you to the centre of the island, past the jungle, to a mysterious empty clearing in the middle. Stand still now at the edge of this clearing. Let your eyes adjust to the dim light.

As the morning light becomes stronger, you watch this space in the centre of the island. Imagine you are standing in the centre of the island, watching and waiting. What can you discover there? Something will come into your imagination. Watch inside your mind. Something will come into this mysterious space.

It will be a surprise, something wonderful, beautiful, something unexpected. See what is happening there, in the centre of the island, see every detail. Watch and wait for your imagination to show you this surprise.

I will be quiet for a moment now. (pause)

The day becomes brighter and hotter. Now it is time to return to your tribe, to your homeland. It is time to leave the centre of the island.

So, as you turn away from the centre of this mysterious space, remember what you saw there. Carefully, you follow the track back towards the beach, past the jungle, across the grass, down the sandy beach.

You slide your canoe down the sand, back to the water, and paddle for home.

Soon, you can start to see your beach, the smoke from the remains of the fire and your homeland.

When you get back to your beach, back to your tribe, you are invited to sketch the surprise that you found in the centre of the mysterious island. People want to know what you saw on your adventure.

So, when you are ready, could you do a quick sketch of the surprise?

Could you write down something about the surprise? What was it?

What strengths does it have?

In what ways is this surprise in the centre of the mysterious island a little bit like you?

STRENGTH VISUALISATION

The Shopping Trip – A Gift for You

This story invites you to imagine you are very wealthy and you have lots of money. So, you can see that for some people this is a very enjoyable story.

Sit comfortably or lie down and relax. You can close your eyes if you wish, if it helps you imagine. Take some deep breaths, and relax as much as you can.

Imagine now you are very, very wealthy. Very, very rich. You are so rich that you could do anything, go anywhere and buy absolutely anything in the whole world. You help others a lot with your wealth. You are very generous; you give to others.

Today you are having a day off from helping others, and you are going on a shopping trip to buy something special for yourself – a wonderful gift just for you!

So, this is your imaginary journey: You have your own jet, of course. See yourself now in your own jet, sipping your favourite drink, in a big comfortable seat, peacefully flying above the clouds.

Remember this is your day to go shopping for yourself. You have lots of money and a special golden credit card, which has no limit!

You issue orders to the pilot to land in a country where you wish to go shopping. I wonder what country would that be? Could you imagine this?

You have a very fast jet, of course, so fast that your pilot is starting to land already. Look out the window of your jet. What do you see? Imagine the countryside.

When you land you see someone is waiting to take you to the shopping place. How do you go to the shopping place? Will it be in a car? On a boat? In a carriage? On horse-back? On a motor bike? Or do you simply walk?

Now you are walking down the street. Are there buildings? Are there any shops? Or, is it an open-air market place? See what comes into your imagination.

Soon you become attracted to one shop. You know this is it! What sort of shop is it? Imagine walking about, looking at what is for sale.

Today you are going to buy yourself a very beautiful, special gift, something of great quality. It could be anything.

Check that you feel good buying something wonderful for yourself. Remember, you have helped others, and today it is your turn.

In your imagination, select what might be the best quality, the thing that attracts you most in the shop. It might be something you have always wanted – or it might be a complete surprise!

Remember, it could be anything! There is no limit! Wait and see what the gift will be.

(pause)

Can you see it clearly in your mind? Just rest and see what it will be. Let your imagination show it.

When you are ready move to the paper and crayons. Sketch the gift you have selected for yourself. Even if you are not good at drawing, quickly sketch something that will remind you of the gift. (pause)

Would you like to talk about the gift, and how it felt to be rich? About the country you went to, or how it felt to buy the gift?

Role-Play of the Gift

Well, this may seem a bit weird, but that gift can tell you something good about yourself!

If you want to relax again and play another imagination game you might find out more about yourself.

So, sit down, relax as much as you can, take a few deep breaths and feel the chair or the carpet beneath you. Feel your breath coming and going.

This may sound strange, but can you imagine you are this gift that you brought for yourself? For a short time you are no longer a person. You are the gift.

I will ask the gift some questions.

If you are comfortable to do it, you can close your eyes and allow a picture of the gift to come back into your mind's eye.

Be interested in how the gift looks and feels. Now let yourself become this gift. Imagine your body changing; change how you are sitting if it helps.

Take a full breath, and feel how it is to be the gift. Would you like to have a picture in your mind of what you – the gift – looks like?

And, feel inside, what you are made of or what is inside you?

Do you – the gift – have a special purpose? What are you for? Could you share that?

What are your strengths?

How would this strength be helpful?

If the gift could talk, what would be its message for you? Does it have anything it would like to say to you? Any advice perhaps? or encouragement?

Now come back to being yourself, and then gently open your eyes. Look about. You are not the gift. You are you now, a person again.

How do you feel now? Did you hear any messages from the gift?

Next to the sketch of the gift, could you write down the most important message from being the gift?

TIME IN NATURE VISUALISATION

Ascent of the Mountain

This activity invites mental imagery of spending time in nature. Participants can recall a place they know, or simply let their imagination picture a scene, guided by the presenter's suggestions.

Take a moment to get comfortable. You can stretch out on the carpet, lean back in the cushions, or sit in a chair.

In this activity you are invited to use lots of imagination. I will invite you to imagine a short journey through some scenes out in nature. You could also remember a real place you have actually been to.

The Ascent

The journey today begins at the foot of a mountain or a very large hill. Take a moment to see in your mind's eye a mountain or hill, one that is not too high, one you could spend time climbing.

You could picture yourself alone setting out on this climbing adventure, or you may like to imagine your best friends are beside you. You are equipped with strong boots, a water bottle, sunscreen, a protective hat and of course some healthy snacks. You begin to slowly walk forward.

The ground is sloping up. At the moment, it is easy going. You stop briefly to admire the scenery. What can you see around you? Are there trees? Rocks? Wild-flowers? Can you see the sky today? Are there clouds? Is it sunny?

Now the path seems narrower, and it is becoming steeper. You might need to take a few deep breaths. You tread carefully. You can see you are higher up now, further up the mountain.

The Summit

As you arrive at the top of the mountain, you stop to look all around you. You take a sip of water. You have a very wide view of the countryside. You made it! Notice the colours of the lands spread out below you. You may see some majestic birds gliding on high. You may hear little but the breeze. There could be houses and roads and people far below.

As you catch your breath, you sit and close your eyes for a moment. You may still clearly feel your heart beating. You relax into a sitting position.

As you sit quietly, imagine you are taking this special time to think about what is most important for you. Take a deep breath, and see what comes into your mind when I ask these questions:

- *What is really important to you in your life at the moment?*
- *Is there something your inner self might be trying to tell you?*

The Descent

When you are ready, imagine you are standing up, stretching, and setting out on the track back home. See yourself walking carefully back down the track.

You might like to recall your thoughts about what is important to you in your life, and get ready to write something about this.

The journey up the mountain is complete now. See if you would like to take a moment to write or draw about your thoughts, feelings and imagination in this activity.

WISDOM VISUALISATION

The Wisest Person on Earth

This activity is another imaginary journey. It is called a visualisation; it invites you to visualise, to imagine a scene in your mind. It uses your imagination to help you find a wise part of you.

Lean back or lie down, and relax as much as you can. Let your body feel supported by the carpet or chair. Breathe in and relax the air out. Let your body melt down, soften, relax. There is nothing to do now, just be with yourself. You may like to close your eyes to help you imagine.

Let a picture come into your mind of yourself in a very beautiful, safe place in nature. Let the picture come to you. It may be a place you know already, or it could be one you make up. See if you are in the open air? Or in a garden? In a park? At the beach? This is a place where you feel safe and happy.

It is a place where you feel comfortable, warm, and relaxed. In your imagination, you look around and see the beauty of the place. Gradually, you see every detail of what is around you.

Now you see a very kind, happy, wise person is in this place with you. This is the wisest person on Earth. This is someone you can trust, someone you could ask for advice. They are there with you in this safe place.

This is the wisest person on Earth. You may know who they are, or you may not.

Look carefully, can you see them in your imagination? Are they old or young? How do they move? Do you notice any special details? Can you see their clothes? What can you tell about this person from their mood?

They are coming closer now. They offer to be your guide, your helper or advisor, for the next few minutes.

See if you can imagine this wise person and you together: Are you standing? Have you found a place to sit?

How do you communicate? Do you speak with words? Or do you just share your thoughts without speaking? How do they respond to you?

This is the wisest person on Earth. What would be the most important question you would want to ask? What is the thing you most want to know about? (pause)

Picture yourself asking the important question now and wait to hear what they say. (pause)

You listen carefully. Listen to their answer to your important question. It might be good to take a deep breath and allow your mind and heart to open to the wisdom of this person. (pause)

Is there anything else you want to tell them or ask of them? Is there anything else they want to say to you?

Tune in, and notice how you feel being with this person, and how it feels to have asked your question.

Now they signal to you that it is time for them to go. They get ready to leave. Are there any last words of advice you ask for as they leave? Are there some last words from them?

How do you say goodbye? See how the wise person leaves now. You watch them go.

Again, take a look at this beautiful place around you. Now breathe the feeling of the beautiful place into you – take it inside with a few deep breaths.

You realise it is also time for you to leave.

So, when you are ready, gently bring your focus back into the room, feel what is beneath you. See if you can stay connected to the feeling of this beautiful, safe place inside you. You might like to move your toes and fingers a little. Let your eyes open gently. Stay quiet for a moment.

Remind yourself of the important question and what the wise person said.

Would you like to write down anything? Remember how it felt to be with the wise person. Could you describe that?

Would you like to draw the safe place and the wise person? If you do, you may like to put the picture up at home and look at it each day for a few weeks, to remember this wisest person on Earth, who is really a part of you!

5 Sitting Still – Doing Nothing

Mindfulness, Meditation and Self-awareness for Young People 9–14 Years

This chapter is designed to support young people from approximately 9 to 14 years. The activities blend skills in self-awareness, relaxation, and slow movement and focus on breath and body, as doorways to developing a meditative and focused state. As with multimodal activities, extensive use is made of imagery, metaphor and visualisation, in an effort to gather participants' attention and support them to find multiple ways to connect and make sense of the activities.

DOI: 10.4324/9781003716501-5

RELAXATION WITH AUTOGENIC PHRASES

Inviting Softness

Ideally participant(s) is/are lying down on soft, carpeted space. Explain that this activity uses imagination and visualisation to send messages of relaxation to the body.

Picture a warm sunny day. You are lying in the shade on soft, warm grass.

Your whole body feels happy and relaxed. Your body is warm and comfortable. Can you imagine that?

Wriggle your body a little and feel the grass underneath. Then you let your back melt down, like warm cheese on a pizza.

It is a quiet day and there is nothing you have to do now. You have plenty of time to be comfortable, relaxed and warm.

Feel your head resting on the soft grass. Notice which parts of your back are resting on the grass. Your back is becoming softer, relaxed and warm.

Your arms can spread out a little. Now your body feels more open – like a flower opening to sunshine.

Your legs are warm and comfortable. They are starting to relax. Your legs can be strong and soft at the same time. They sometimes feel like tiger's legs. Now they can be still and let the grass and the earth beneath provide support.

Begin to feel your strength and feel how good it is to let go of thoughts and worries. Your body is warm and comfortable, soft and open. See if you could stay with this focus inside yourself for a moment. (pause)

See if your mind might like to send you a picture of something from nature that shows some of the way you feel inside now.

When you feel ready, bring your awareness back into the room. Would you like to draw something that goes with how you felt inside after this activity?

RELAXATION THROUGH VIBRATION

The Humming Tunnel

Some people like to hum when they are happy, sometimes making up a little tune or humming a tune they know and like. For this activity, we will use humming to help us relax. This might not seem exciting at first, because the humming can be very, very simple. You don't have to speak, you don't have to sing, you simply hum.

So, to start, stand up, shake your body – just like a dog might shake if it jumped into the waves at the beach and then wanted to dry off quickly.

And now settle into a comfortable chair or sit on a cushion. Take a deep breath, and let your body relax as much as it can.

You might like to close your eyes to help you concentrate. As we play with this humming activity, see if you can let go of the temptation to be interested in what is happening outside of you, outside of this room.

This may sound a little strange at first, but could you imagine a tunnel right through the middle of you, from the top of your head, down to your toes? This is the humming tunnel.

Breathe a full breath in, without forcing it. And on the out-breath, let your body go soft, and picture in your mind that the air is flowing down that tunnel.

Imagine your breath pouring down that imaginary tunnel past your throat, through your heart, through your tummy and flowing into two channels, one down each leg, all the way to your toes.

Imagine you could watch your breath travelling through you, and you could feel it moving through the tunnel.

Let's imagine this now, while we take ten slow, full breaths. First breath: comes in, and then as the air flows out imagine it going down the tunnel, not out your nose. Second breath: bring it in, and then out through the tunnel. And the third breath, imagining it flowing out down the tunnel through the middle of you. And just keep going until you get to ten breaths.

Let the breath be full, but gentle.

Now let's add some humming with each out-breath. You breathe in, and hum as the air flows out. You try a humming sound right now. You have a go – do it with me. Slowly breathe in, and hum out the breath.

Where can you feel that sound in your body? I can feel it in my mouth and throat a little. You try it again. And I will see if I can hear you. (pause) *OK?*

Now add the humming as you breathe out, as you imagine the breath going down through the tunnel inside you. Imagine the humming and the breath dancing down that tunnel through the middle of you.

Let's do this together for a moment. And see if we can make the humming a little louder. You can play with the sound, make it go deeper or higher, or louder then softer. Let's try again. That's great.

Now try a little softer humming.

Perhaps the humming can loosen up your worries and it may even vibrate your muscles a little. Could you imagine sending the humming down the tunnel to your tummy right now? See if you could send the humming down the middle of your body. I wonder how that feels for you? Let's do it together.

(If you are doing this with people around you who are also humming, it might seem funny to hear all the sounds in the room.)

Now, imagine the humming is vibrating down your right arm, as if there was a small humming tunnel through your shoulder, past your elbow, down through your hand and out your fingertips. Try that now with a few breaths. Breathing in, and then imagine the humming and the breath sliding down through your right arm, through the tunnel, through your shoulder, past your elbow, down through your hand and out through your fingertips.

Now turn your attention to your right leg. See if you could try sending the humming down all the way down through your right leg.

And now your left leg. Big breath in, and imagine you are breathing out through a tunnel in your left leg, and you are sending the humming there as you breathe out. Long, full, humming down through the left leg.

And now, see if you can send the humming down your left arm, into your fingers. Breathe in, and imagine the breath and the humming going down through your shoulder, down past your elbow, through your wrist, your hand and out your fingers.

Now again humming through the middle of your body a few times. Imagine that tunnel through the centre of you. So, let's do that together. A big breath in, and humming through the middle.

Remember, you are humming gently as your breath goes out, as the breath goes down through the tunnel. Keep imagining that humming is sliding around and around down the tunnel, through the middle of you.

It could feel a little bit like the humming is washing away some worries and waking up your energy.

Imagine sending the humming down to your tummy again. See if you could send the humming there.

Now move your focus to your right arm. We will go around the body again, sending the humming through all the different parts. So, imagine the humming and the breath going down your right arm, as if there was a small tunnel through your shoulder, past your elbow, down through your hand and out your fingertips.

Try sending the humming down your right leg now.

And now the left leg.

And now send the humming down through your left arm, all the way through into your fingertips.

And again, use the humming tunnel. See if you can hum through the middle of your body a few times. Breath comes in through your nose, and the breath and the humming move together – imagine them going through an invisible tunnel through your throat, your heart, your belly, down through your legs, and out through your arms, your fingers and your toes.

And let's rest now. Could you take a moment to sit still and do nothing?

Can you feel where the humming has been? See if the humming has made a difference to how you feel inside.

What do you notice? Are there any colours or feelings or words that could go with how you feel inside you now?

Would you like to draw or write something now about using the humming tunnel?

Remember, you can use humming whenever you want. It can be a good way to help you wash away some of the worries, and feel more calm.

GUIDED IMAGERY FOR SELF-ESTEEM

Your Power Animal

This activity can support participants to find a sense of supportive strengths within, and to carry an internal image (and external drawing as a reinforcer) of their strength as a reminder that they do have resources to cope with their worries.

Take a moment to get comfortable. This activity takes place in your imagination.

Some people say that all of life is like a journey. We are all given strengths to face our fears, to face problems and worries, and to make our lives wonderful and exciting. But sometimes this strength is hidden inside us. This activity can help us call it out of hiding.

If you like, we can now go on an imaginary journey to find the help we need. The help will come from a magic power creature, a spirit animal, bird or fish. This spirit creature is waiting for us in a distant land. This land lies deep down in your own imagination.

To arrive at this deep secret land in our own imagination, we will need to take a great dive and swim down through the waters of our thoughts and feelings to arrive at the place where the creature is waiting. It might be good to take a few deep breaths to gather your energy, ready for the dive.

Now let's go! Can you picture yourself taking a deep dive? It is like leaping off the top of your own head, and swimming down and down to the mysterious land of imagination deep inside you. (pause)

The land is in sight. We come into shallow waters. There is a huge cave. Look around inside your imagination. What can you see? What sort of landscape is around you?

Find your special place to wait for the power animal. This magical creature will appear just for you. Let yourself become quiet and still.

See how your power animal appears. Does it swim? Fly? Hop? Run? See it as clearly as you can, every detail of its body. It is calm and friendly. It moves closer to you. It wants to communicate. At first, you cannot understand its language. But this is a magic animal, a special magic spirit creature, so it turns you into its twin.

Feel yourself becoming the same as this magic animal. Could you move a bit, make its sounds? Feel your skin, is it fur, or feathers, or fins? Feel the animal's special strengths flowing into you.

Now you listen. It is giving you a special message and passing on to you its strength. Listen to its message. (pause)

Now it is time to say goodbye. See your animal go. As it goes, you become a person on the outside – but inside you keep the feeling of that strength.

You have a big leap ahead. Picture yourself now. Leaping up out of the land of your imagination, and swimming up and up. You are heading back into your whole self, and back into this room.

When you feel ready, open your eyes and move to your drawing and writing material. What might you like to draw or write? You could draw your power creature. You could draw something to go with how you feel now after the activity. You might like to write down the message from your power creature.

MOVEMENT MEDITATION

Bare Feet, Slow Walking

Before the start of this activity, have some large sheets of paper and some crayons ready. Participants take off their shoes, and stand on the paper and draw around each foot, so they have an outline on the paper of the shape of their feet. Keep the paper and crayons nearby to use at the end of the activity.

This is a moving meditation. We usually think of meditation as sitting still, but this one involves walking around the room slowly. It will be best to make sure you have some clear space in the room. Make sure there is nothing you could trip over. Also, for this meditation, do keep your eyes open when you are moving!

Worries swirl around our minds, around our heads. This activity can help us turn away from worries by sending our focus down to our feet. You may also like to try the activity while walking slowly outside the room. Bare feet help you feel the floor and the ground beneath you.

We will be walking – not to arrive anywhere – but to study what happens inside while we walk. Usually we are concerned with getting somewhere fast. For this moving meditation, there is nowhere to go, and we go there slowly.

So, to begin, stand up and stretch as much as you can. Take a few deep breaths and relax the air out, let it flow out by itself.

Begin to walk slowly around the room. Walk very, very slowly. Keep your eyes open.

Begin to feel the floor under your feet. Is it smooth or rough? Is there carpet? Are you on floorboards? Is the floor warm or cool?

See if you can relax your whole body as you walk along. Can you drop any tension in your neck? Allow your shoulders to relax. Let your body take some full breaths. Allow your belly to be relaxed.

As you walk, turn your focus to your knees. Send your attention inside to your knees for a moment. How are they? Tight? Relaxed? Can you simply notice the movement in your knees as you walk?

Now slow down your walking, but keep moving forward. You might be moving around the room in a large circle. Take a large breath in, and let the air relax out.

Become aware of your feet as you move, feel how your toes and heels touch the floor. Which part of your feet touches the floor first? For a moment, focus on the way your feet move and make contact with the floor. (pause)

Is it possible to walk and feel your ankles moving at the same time? Can you practice walking and feeling your feet and ankles move over the floor for a while? Keep your eyes open, but try not to focus on anything outside of you.

I will be quiet for a moment, and you practice feeling the way your feet touch the floor.

If it is good weather outside, and if it is easy and safe to go outside, there could be some slow walking practice outside. This can increase participants' experiences of sensations in the feet.

Try not to look around you too much. Just keep focusing inside your body on the way your feet touch the ground. See if you can feel the temperature of the ground, and the textures under your feet, the hardness or softness of the ground.

Try a little more of this walking meditation, but let your walking become slower and slower. Moving so slowly now that no one could see you moving.

Come to a quiet stop. Be still. You could close your eyes for a moment. And just feel the floor under your feet. Could you stand still and do nothing? Practice being as still as you can for a moment. Can you connect your awareness to the inside of you? Can you still feel your feet?

When you are ready, open your eyes, take a deep breath and move to the paper and the crayons. On the outlines of your feet, you could use colours and lines to show what you noticed in your feet.

You may also like to write down one or two things you noticed as you tried this activity. What stood out to you?

There are many times when we want to feel more calm. When we are calm, we can think more clearly, feel more positive and have more control over our decisions.

Slow walking, while you practice the skill of keeping your focus inside, is a way to become more calm.

MOVEMENT MEDITATION

Slower Than a Snail

This is a slow-motion activity. Sometimes on television you can see basketball players send the ball through the hoop very slowly, so you can see each moment of the play. Sometimes we see documentaries of animals and birds moving super slow. This activity is like that.

Have you ever watched a snail in the garden move? They are very slow compared to the way we rush about. Imagine you live in a world where the fastest thing is a snail! Everything moves slowly in this world. Everyone here is very patient, and everything happens so slowly.

When you first arrive in this strange slow world it looks as if everything is still. But, soon you realise it is the slow-motion world. Luckily the days here are very long, or nothing would get done.

When you visit, you want to try out this slow motion. Could you do it? We may have to really pay attention to move slowly, and not speed up to our usual pace. So, you try to go as slow as everyone else in this world. If you moved at your normal speed, no one in the slow-motion world would see you. You would be just a blur to them.

To begin, stand up, stretch for a moment then let your body relax. Use your imagination to help you move in very slow motion, and get ready to visit this slow-motion world.

First, tune in to your neck. Let your neck relax, allow your chin to move slowly down towards your chest. Let this happen very slowly, as if you were in a slow-motion movie. Feel what is happening in the muscles in your neck, as your head moves slowly down.

With your breathing, let the old air flow out, and notice how you fill again with new air.

Let your neck move slowly all the way down and then up – slowly – so it is tilting back. Then, again, flowing down and up, softly like clouds floating across the sky. Then move your head back slowly to its normal position.

Sometimes this meditation brings out our impatience – we want to speed up. We want to get on with it! But in this slower-than-a-snail world slow is good.

Tune in to your arms. Slowly raise your arms up in front of you, until they are about level with shoulders. Imagine they rise up by themselves, very slowly. Could you do it even slower? Then slowly relax, let your arms fall again, but very gently and slowly.

Feel how you have to add tension in the muscles as your arms rise up. They are rising as slowly as grass growing. And notice how you let go as your arms float down again until there is no muscle tension at all.

There is no "right" or "wrong" way to do this, and you cannot make a mistake.

Tune in to your legs now. Begin to slowly bend your knees. Feel the changes in your muscles as your knees bend. Your knees are bending so slowly, like ice melting on a warm day. Feel the way you have to add strength as you rise up again. Try this again, letting your knees bend, so your body moves down a little. Really notice the changes inside.

Let's practice snail-speed movements some more.

Tune in again to your neck. Tune in to your neck. Let your neck relax. Allow your chin to move slowly down towards your chest. Let it happen very slowly, as if you were in a slow-motion movie. Feel what is happening in your neck muscles.

Let yourself breathe out the old air, and fill again with new air.

Let your neck move slowly all the way down, and then all the way up, so it is tilting back. Can you feel each little change in your neck? Can you feel a little temptation to speed up?

Now, slowly raise your arms up in front of you – very slowly – until they are about level with your shoulders, then slowly let go, let the arms fall again, but very very slowly. Feel how you have to use some tension as your arms rise up, and the way you have to let go as they slowly flow down again.

Relax your arms, and tune in to your legs and knees now. Slowly bend your knees. Feel your body letting go as you move down. Feel the way you have to add strength to your legs as you rise up again.

I wonder if your arms and knees could move together? Your arms rise slowly up as your knees bend down. Each time you come up in your knees feel how tall you are.

Keep allowing your breath to release. Keep the movements all very slow. Notice if you feel impatient – that is normal. Return to moving slowly.

Now, could you let your head join the movement. And let your whole body flow into any movement you like, a slow snail dance. You don't have to plan how to move; you just let it happen. See what movements would feel good.

Get ready to fit in with the slow-motion world. Move your whole body slowly like a snail, or like a cloud floating across the sky. Your neck is moving. Your arms are moving. Your legs are moving.

(pause)

Now, let all the movement stop. Lie down, or sit back in a chair – for a moment, you rest. Feel what it is like inside you now. I will be quiet. See how it feels inside your body now. Could you be still and do nothing?

Practice being still for a moment, and see what you notice.

(pause)

When you are ready, come back into this world, look around this room.

You may like to take a moment to draw or write something about how it felt to do the slow-motion meditation.

GROUNDING VISUALISATION

Finding Strength

This activity is especially useful for young people who feel overwhelmed or vulnerable to outside forces. It can support connection to resilience.

Stand up, stretch a little, then let your eyes close. Feel your feet firmly on the floor. Take a few deep breaths and relax them out.

See if you can picture this: Your energy reaches down through the floor, down into the earth beneath. Imagine feeling the soil on your feet, really imagining the touch of the soil, the cool, brown earth against the soles of your feet.

Now, could you imagine there are tiny little roots growing out of the bottom of your feet – reaching down towards the earth – going deeper into the earth – becoming thicker now – much thicker – very big thick roots? These roots are becoming stronger now – very strong, deep roots – they go right down deeply into the earth. These roots can hold you firm.

A strong wind begins to blow. Feel it moving through your branches, bending your limbs, making you sway this way and that. Feel how your strong roots hold you steady, even though the wind tries to blow you over.

You are a strong tree, you are growing in a valley, it has been raining hard for some days. Now there's a stream of water coming down the valley. Feel the water rushing by. Feel how your roots are held firmly to the earth.

You are firmly in your place. Breathe into that strength, your solidness, your connectedness to the earth.

Would you like to draw a picture of yourself as the strong tree? Could you draw something that can remind you of yourself as the strong tree?

When you are ready, would you like to talk about how you feel now?

Are there things that happen in your life where having these strong roots would be helpful?

REVIEW AND REFLECT

Not Yesterday, Not Tomorrow, Just Now

This meditation helps us first recall what happened during the day, and then it encourages us to let go of what has happened. So, it is good to do it late in the day. This is especially useful when you have been stressed, or just "had a really bad day". It is refreshing to let go of thinking about the problems and worries of the day, and perhaps enjoy the best moments.

Can you sit in a comfortable chair, or on a thick cushion with crossed legs, for this activity? Many people find that if they close their eyes it helps them focus on the activity. It is helpful to begin by taking in a few deep breaths.

See if you can go through the pictures of each step of your day in your mind. Follow each step of the day, each feeling in your day, recall each person you met, all the way up until now. See if you can remember all the things that you were doing, saying, feeling and hoping today.

Can you remember yourself at home early this morning?

Take a full breath. Then tune in to your memories of the day. It is as if you were watching your own home video in your mind. Can you remember:

- *When you were waking up?*
- *Your first feeling about the day?*
- *Can you remember getting out of bed?*
- *When you got dressed?*
- *When you were eating breakfast?*
- *Can you remember going to work (or school)?*
- *Can you remember who you were with?*
- *And all the places you went today?*
- *Can you remember things that you heard, and what you said?*
- *What was not so good in your day?*
- *And what did you enjoy most during the day?*

Watch inside your mind: What stands out from the day?

Take another few slow full breaths, and relax as much as you can on the out-breath.

When we are stressed, we think about the past, or worry about what is ahead. This meditation we are exploring now is simply called "Not Yesterday, Not Tomorrow, Just Now". That means we focus on each new moment. After remembering the day, we focus on what is happening right now. We turn our minds away from the past or the future.

So, to begin the next step, could you focus on your body and how it feels inside at the moment? Can you tell which mood you are in? Is there a mood?

What do you notice at the moment – in your head? Or in any part of your body?

Is there any part of you that you can notice more clearly? Tune in and see: Maybe your chest? Your belly? Hands? Your legs? Or face? What stands out to you in this moment? (pause)

See if you can watch your thoughts floating past, like clouds across the sky. Is this possible? How could this be done? (pause)

It may help to keep letting thoughts float away if you also focus on letting your body relax a bit more. Could you let your body melt a little?

Watch inside, right now. Become a watcher who looks inside, who simply sees what is inside you in this moment. (pause)

Let your focus move to the way you breathe. Notice your breathing coming and going. With each breath, pay attention to the little movements in your body. (pause)

Let your focus move into the middle of your chest. Feel the rise and fall of your breath. (pause)

Every time you think about something else, turn back to this moment, to what you can notice inside. Start again to see what you notice inside you, in this moment. Tuning in – not out.

I will be quiet now. See if you can continue to feel your breath moving and notice how your body feels. Keep turning back to breath and body if new thoughts start up. Could you be still and do nothing?

Now it is time to bring your attention back to the room. When you are ready, you may like to stretch a bit.

Could you use colours and shapes or pictures to show what you noticed while you were sitting still? You might like to show how it felt to have your thoughts and attention pulled away to the past or future. Or how it felt when you were focused right here, right now, in this moment.

MENTAL IMAGERY FOR SOMATIC EXPERIENCE

My Four-Storey Building

This activity is designed to elicit imagery that can emerge from bringing focus to areas of the body. As usual, the speed of presentation can be determined by the attention span of participants. Frequent use of pauses while participants reflect and sense will be helpful.

Invite participants to fill a large page with a drawing of a profile of a four-storey apartment building, number the apartments with the top one being 4. Have crayons ready, so they can draw something on each floor as the visualisation progresses.

You might like to sit cross-legged on cushions, or in a relaxed and balanced way in a chair. As with so many activities that help us explore our inner world, you might like to start with eyes closed.

This may sound strange, but could you imagine yourself as an apartment block with four storeys? There are four apartments (or flats) inside where people could live. Through the middle is a lift. It can stop at each floor. There are different things happening on each floor. You can imagine moving around inside the four apartments, which are really all inside you.

Mostly, you live on the fourth floor. Could you picture yourself there now? It is the floor with big glass windows, where you can look out to see all the business of the world around you. This apartment is in your head! Could you bring your focus to your head? How does it feel inside your head at the moment?

So, take a look around this apartment you spend most time in. What is here? Thoughts? Bits and pieces of today, this morning, things from yesterday, plans for tomorrow? It is usually cluttered with thoughts. Take a moment to look around inside and see if you can notice the busy thoughts. (pause) *Could you draw something onto the page for the fourth floor?* (pause)

Actually, you may have been living on the fourth floor so long you have almost forgotten what is on the other floors! So today is a day to explore. You can go down the list to check out what is on the third floor.

Now imagine you are moving to the lift. Grab your torch and step in. Press the button marked 3. The door slides closed. You go down.

The doors open. This floor is lower down inside your throat and chest area. This is the apartment where sounds are made. It is the place where feelings are often made. It is a place of comfortable and uncomfortable feelings.

Take a deep breath and tune into your chest area, then imagine you are looking around there. Do you need the torch? What is here? There could be some feelings, and maybe some sounds or words that have not been spoken yet? Pleasant moods, uncomfortable moods? Loud words, whispered words? (pause) *Could you draw something onto the page that goes with the third floor?* (pause)

Now imagine you are moving to the centre of the main room again, to the lift. You press the button marked 2. The doors slide closed. You go down. Again, when the doors open, it seems dark at first.

The second floor is lower down, it is in your belly area. What type of apartment is this? How does it look? Imagine you are looking through the rooms here on the second floor.

There could be some feelings stored here that have been hiding, out of sight.

See if you can take a deep breath, and tune into your belly area now. At the same time, see if you can imagine any feelings that could be stored here. (pause) *Could you draw something on the page that goes with the third floor?* (pause)

Finally, see if you could imagine you are moving to the lift again. You step in. Press the button marked 1. The door slides closed. You go down.

The door opens. This floor is lower down inside your legs and feet. This is the apartment where strength can be stored, where actions and movements roam free.

Take a deep breath and tune into your legs and feet, then imagine you are looking around inside them. What is here? There could be some action or movements that want to be freer. (pause) *Could you draw something on the page that goes with the first floor?* (pause)

When you feel ready, look over the building. See what you have expressed on the page. Is there anything that looks most interesting to you? Are there some areas you would like to talk about?

SOMATIC FOCUSED MEDITATION

An Apple in My Hand

This is a very quiet and still meditation. This is a time for you to learn to pay attention, to focus, to what is happening inside you.

During each day we spend so much time looking at everything around us, and sometimes worrying about what others think about us, and what's going to happen in the future. So this is a time to practice noticing what is inside us right now, and letting go of worries.

This meditation uses an apple to help us concentrate on what is inside us; to turn from focusing outside of ourselves to the inside. Some people call it "The Apple Meditation". So you will need an apple, but please do not eat the apple until after the meditation!

Find a comfortable way to sit. Meditation is usually done sitting up. Let your hands rest on your knees, with your palms open and facing up. Put the apple in the hand that you usually write with. It may help you concentrate if you close your eyes, and if you take two deep breaths before you start.

Begin with your focus on the hand that is holding the apple. Feel the weight of the apple. Focus on the temperature of the apple. What do you notice – is the apple cooler or warmer than your hand?

Can you also feel the texture of the skin of the apple with your fingers?

See if you can relax your hand as much as possible, just keeping your hand shaped around the apple so it doesn't roll away.

Focus on what is in your hand – the temperature of the apple, the texture of its skin, and its weight. Let your breath come and go freely, in a relaxed way.

Now slowly move the apple to the other hand.

Feel the weight of the apple again in the other hand. Focus on the temperature, the texture and the weight of the apple. Is the apple cooler or warmer than your hand?

Can you feel the texture of the skin of the apple? See if you can relax your hand as much as possible, without the apple rolling away. Focus for a moment on how the apple feels in your hand.

In meditation, it is normal to notice thoughts, ideas, floating into your mind, distracting you. Try to keep coming back to focus on your hand and the apple in it.

See if you can let thoughts float away, take a deep breath, and start focusing on your hand again. (pause)

Now, move the apple slowly to the other hand.

Bring your attention, your focus to the feeling in your hand, to the hand that is holding the apple. Can you feel the temperature of the air on the skin of your hand that is holding the apple?

Can you feel the area where your hand rests on your knee?

Turn your attention now to the inside of your hand. Is it possible to feel the blood flowing inside your hand? Can you feel the temperature of your hand?

Can you notice the energy inside your hand? Some people feel a tiny tingle or buzz of energy, some feel a warmth. Sometimes it just feels very alive inside.

Put the apple down now. Imagine that it is still there, and pretend to place it in the other hand.

Bring your focus to the feeling in the hand that would be holding the apple.

Can you feel the temperature of the air on the skin of the hand that would be holding the apple?

Can you feel the area where your hand rests on your knee? Turn your attention now to the inside of your hand. Is it possible to feel the blood flowing inside? Can you feel the temperature of your hand? Can you notice the energy inside your hand?

I know this is a lot of questions. So I will be quiet for a while, and you continue imagining the apple and your focus in one hand, then after a minute or two, swap to the other hand. (pause)

See if you can turn your attention to focus on the middle of your body now. Can you tune in to the movement of breathing in your chest? Stay with that for a while. Simply feel your chest rising and falling.

What is it like to be more at home, inside yourself? Could you sit still and do nothing?

(pause)

As you bring your awareness back to the room, see if you can also stay connected with your inner world.

I hope that after this, when you see an apple, you might remember this meditation, and again imagine the apple in your hand.

If you wish, you could spend some time now with drawing, or writing, something that goes with how you feel now.

And later, if you wish, you could eat the apple.

MINDFULNESS BREATH MEDITATION

The Air Flows In and Out

This is a sitting still type of meditation. It seems very simple at first. It is really a way to stretch the time you can focus inside yourself, and get to know what is happening in your body, in your feelings and in your energy.

You may have to let go of the temptation to worry about what is happening around you, or to enjoy daydreams. This meditation asks that you keep bringing your focus back to two main areas inside you – your chest and your belly.

Sit comfortably in a chair or on a cushion. Allow your body to relax as much as it can. Take a few breaths and relax them out.

To begin, let your body become still. You can wriggle a little now to help you settle in, then try not to move. Be as still as you can.

Move your attention on your chest, the area of your body where your heart is beating, keeping life moving inside. Put one hand on your upper chest for a moment. Tune in there under your hand. Feel it rise and fall as your breath comes and goes.

(pause)

Now move your attention down to your belly. Put your other hand there. See if you can feel your belly from the outside – under your hand – and also from inside. Let your belly relax as much as it can. Does it move as you breathe?

Now I am going to invite you to keep moving your focus from your chest to your belly. Move your attention to your chest as you breathe in. Then drop your focus down to your belly on the out-breath.

Your attention will simply fall and rise between the heart area and the belly area, along with your breathing.

Let your breathing stay natural and relaxed. Let your hands relax now. Let them rest.

(pause)

We will focus for a while, feeling first the chest and how it moves a little with the breath. Feel that from the inside, then focus on the belly. See if you can tell if your belly also moves a bit with the breathing.

There is nothing else to do. Simply stay quietly focused inside yourself, moving your awareness between the two focus areas – your chest on the in-breath, and then your belly on the out-breath.

(pause)

Every time a new thought comes into your mind, and you realise it has taken you away from the activity, sigh out your breath – as if you were sighing out the thoughts that slip into your mind. Let those thoughts flow away with your breath, then begin again. In this activity, it is normal to begin again and again.

So, time to practice. Breath flows in – you tune in to your heart area.

Breath flows out, and you let your focus drop to your belly area. It is very simple. See if you can keep working with that.

If you notice any thoughts – like "what is supposed to happen?" or "this is boring", try to smile. We knew this might happen. And just start again. Let the thoughts go past.

Breath flows in – you tune in to your heart area. Breath flows out, and you let your focus drop down to your belly area. Your breath will come and go. Practice bringing your thoughts, your focus back. Could you sit still now and do nothing?

(pause)

When you are ready, bring your awareness back into the room.

Is there a way you would like to express what you noticed, or how you feel now? – For example, through writing, or drawing, or through talking about it with someone?

MINDFULNESS PRACTICE

The Sounds around Me

Before we get started on this activity, take a moment to sit still and simply experience your breath coming and going, and notice any sensations in the body.

The aim of this mindfulness activity is to listen to sounds around us, and at the same time return to awareness of breath and body. We will try to let thoughts float by as much as possible, knowing it is quite normal for thoughts to wander and take our focus away to the past or future. Can we be content to keep re-focusing on breath, body and listening to the sounds?

- *So, find a way to sit that feels balanced, and allow your awareness to expand from breath and body sensation, to hearing the sounds around you.*
- *Bring your attention to the ears and then allow the awareness to open and expand, so that there is receptiveness to sounds as they arise, whenever they arise.*
- *There is no need to go searching for sounds or listening for any particular sounds. As best you can, simply open your mind so that it is receptive to sounds from all directions – whether they are in front, behind, to the side, above or below.* (pause)
- *See if you can open to all sounds around you, and let go of thinking about the sounds and what made them. Be aware of sounds and of the spaces between sounds, aware of any silence.*
- *As best you can, be aware of sounds directly, without discussing about them in your head. When you find that you are thinking about the sounds, reconnect, as best you can, with your breath and direct awareness of the sounds, rather than analysing them.* (pause)
- *If you notice that your awareness is no longer focused on sounds, gently acknowledge where your mind has moved to, and reconnect with your breathing and body awareness, and then return your focus back to sounds.*
- *If you notice thoughts intrude, acknowledge them without getting involved, then return focus to the sounds around you, no matter how quiet, faint or indistinct, or simple hear the silence.* (pause)
- *Our practice right now involves gently and consistently returning focus to sounds.*
- *Continue to practice for a few minutes.* (long pause)
- *Take a moment now to bring your focus to your internal state.*
- *When you are ready, slowly expand your awareness to include the room again, without abandoning your internal awareness. See if your body would like to move a little.*
- *On a large sheet of paper, write a few words or phrases that go with your internal experience. When you feel ready, could you arrange these words into a statement? A headline? Or perhaps a poem?*

GRATITUDE REFLECTIONS

My Gratitude Memories

Have pen, paper and crayons or coloured pencils available. This activity arose from positive psychology and positive writing research (see page 19). It aims to reconnect participants with, and encourage them to express, moments of joy and gratitude. These recollections can be used as a resource for well-being.

For this activity, you will be invited to relax as much as you can, and to take a few deep breaths, and tune in to yourself, into your inner world of thoughts, feelings and memories. Then you will be invited to remember some happy experiences (pause).

So, take a few deep breaths, and tune into your inner world as best you can. See if you can take a moment to remember any people in your life you are grateful for. These would be people you feel pleased and thankful about when you think of them. See who comes to mind. (pause) *These might be people who have added happiness and joy to your life. See if you can remember who they are, when you were with them, and how it felt to be with them.* (pause)

Next, take a deep breath, and see if you can remember a place in your life, or anywhere in the world, where you felt some happiness, joy or wonder. This would be a place where you had a feeling of expansion, delight, where you felt uplifted and joyful. (pause)

See if it is possible to recall the places, the scenery, sights and sounds that were around you when you were with a person you are grateful for, or when you felt some wonder and joy. And, is it possible to recall the way you felt in your body at that time? (pause)

Are there any colours, lines or shapes or pictures that might best show your memory of this person or place? When you are ready, could you express these on the art paper?

Are there some keywords that might sum up or describe the experience? Allow words to bubble up by themselves. You could also write these on the page. (pause)

Would you like to finish these sentence starters? It could be with a word or two, it could be a full sentence:

- *I am most grateful for...*
- *A very happy place for me...*
- *Recalling this could be most helpful when...*

Are there any times when reviewing these memories, art and writing could be helpful?

SITTING MEDITATION

In My Bubble – Sitting Still, Doing Nothing

Some people may think it is weird to sit still, doing nothing. But getting to know what is happening inside you is an important exercise. What you learn here could be very helpful for you throughout your life. Learning to meditate can be frustrating, but it can also help you let go of worries, stresses and upsets.

Meditation can help you find confidence and a feeling of strength.

For meditations like this, it is usually best to be sitting up, in a comfortable chair or on a cushion on the floor with your legs crossed. What would be comfortable for you?

I wanted to call this a simple meditation. But that is not quite right, because meditation usually feels difficult at first. When we try to be quiet and still, we usually notice that we are not quiet and still. We start talking in our mind, or we listen to things going on around us.

Usually, we can only pay attention to what is happening inside us for a very short time. But that is what meditation is all about, trying to focus inside for longer, as if for a while we could stay inside our own bubble, letting go of the world outside.

So, if you notice you are not listening, or you are thinking about yesterday or tomorrow, or wondering what people outside are saying or doing, or if you notice you are feeling a bit bored, all you have to do is take in a big breath, and start to pay attention again. It doesn't matter how often you start again.

So, let's start now.

Close your eyes and just notice your breath coming and going.

See if you can feel your heart beating inside.

Let your body be as relaxed as it can. Let your mind focus on feeling what is happening in your body now.

The main effort in meditation is to keep coming back to paying attention to the world inside you. It is as if you are on a safari, travelling through your inner land, watching the scenery, watching what is happening. You try to stay alert.

There are two things that will help: feeling your breath come and go, and feeling your body and the energy inside it. I will remind you to come back to putting your attention on these two areas – breath and body.

Now, allow yourself to relax a little more, without going floppy:

- *Let your neck relax and be a little soft at the back.*
- *Let your shoulders drop.*
- *Allow a full breath to flow in by itself, and then relax.*
- *Can you let your tummy relax?*
- *Can your legs and feet relax?*

Let your breathing relax. Don't try to do anything with your breathing. Just watch how your body does the breathing all by itself! See which parts move? Where does the air go?

You are simply watching inside now, as if you were in a bubble, not getting tangled up in what you notice.

Are any thoughts or pictures in your mind? Could you let these go? Are there any feelings happening at the moment? Could you focus on breathing again? And see what you notice in your body?

Simply be aware of all this, and turn your focus onto your body and your breathing again.

Nothing else: breathing, body.

Again, allow a little bit more relaxation:

- *let your neck relax and be soft at the back*
- *let your shoulders relax*
- *let your tummy be soft*
- *let your legs and feet relax.*

I will be quiet for a few more minutes, see if you can keep coming back to notice what is happening inside. There is nothing else to do, just sitting still. You are noticing your breathing and your body. Could you sit still and do nothing? (pause)

Now, slowly and gently move your toes and fingers a little. Stretch a bit, and when you are ready let your eyes open. Try to stay in touch with the world inside you as you look outside the bubble to the outer world again.

You could take some time to draw how you feel now, or to draw any pictures that floated into your mind while you were sitting still.

You can create this bubble any time. You can do short practices and longer practices. You can use these instructions to help you, over and over.

See if you can begin to enjoy sitting still and doing nothing.

Good luck!

6 Tuning In, Taking Time, Caring for Self

Mindfulness, Reflection and Self-compassion for Adolescents and Adults

This chapter is designed to support older adolescents and adults. The meditative activities develop skills in self-awareness, reflection, self-compassion and mindful focus, as doorways to deepening relaxation, presence and well-being. Again, imagery is offered to support engagement and to communicate more directly to the body. Imagery involving nature is offered, as connection with the outdoors (even recalling it) has been shown to bring feelings of well-being.

Introducing Mindfulness: Some Necessary Attitudes

One of the pioneers of mindfulness in the West, and the original researcher showing the positive effects of mindfulness practice, was Jon Kabat-Zinn (2013). He observed that people are usually caught up in distracting thoughts, they:

- *Rush through activities without being attentive to them*
- *Break and spill things because of inattention, thinking about something else*
- *Do not notice feelings of discomfort or tension*
- *Find themself preoccupied with the future or past*
- *Eat without being aware of eating*
- *Drive home and on arrival, wondering how they got there, etc.*

Jon Kabat-Zinn recommended that if we wish to change, to explore mindfulness, we should adopt several necessary attitudes. Let's take a moment to hear and discuss some of these and what they might mean for us.

- *Aim to increase self-understanding and wisdom.*
- *Pay attention on purpose. Intend to observe what is happening both inside us and outside us.*
- *Aim to let go of what we think we know about ourselves, and keep learning.*
- *Become aware of any automatic self-judgement about our practice and what we observe. For example, it is normal to recognise that we are distracted by continuous thoughts. We should aim to let go of the content of thoughts and let them float by.*

DOI: 10.4324/9781003716501-6

- *Our effort should be to open to each moment, experience each moment, rather than hurry on towards the future.*
- *Aim to be a beginner, not an expert. Observe our inner and outer world as if for the first time. Get used to starting again and again.*
- *Let go of our efforts to achieve something, and practice being present to each moment just as it is.*
- *The practice of observing the way breath comes and goes in each moment forms the foundation of many mindfulness practices.*

SOMATIC FOCUS GROUNDING

Body Scan

This activity supports connection with the body through moving attention through the body. The re-focusing on the various areas of the body supports an ability to refresh intentional, focused awareness.

Invite participants to prepare a large body outline on art paper and have crayons ready.

- *Lie down on the carpet, with a pillow under your head. Make yourself as comfortable as you can, lying on your back. Allow your eyes to close gently to help you keep your focus inside.*
- *This activity can help you build the skill of connecting with your body, and better understanding what it might be communicating to you, and what it needs. The aim is not to make your body relax, but connect with any tensions you find and befriend them with your awareness.*
- *Take a few moments to get in touch with the movement of your breath, feel it coming and going.* (pause)
- *See if you can bring your awareness to the sensations in your body, especially to the touch or pressure, where your body makes contact with the carpet.*
- *On each out-breath, see if you can allow yourself to let go, to sink a little deeper into the carpet.* (pause)
- *We are trying out this activity in order to generate curiosity, to experiment, see what could happen. Remind yourself of the intention to bring awareness to any sensations you detect, not to change anything, as you focus your attention on each part of the body.*
- *To start, bring your awareness to the sensations in the lower belly, becoming aware of the changes in sensations as you breathe in, and as you breathe out. Take a few minutes to feel these sensations that come from the movement of breath in your belly.* (pause)
- *Now bring the focus of your awareness down the left leg, into the left foot, and bring that awareness out to the toes. Focus on the toes of the left foot, noticing the sensations you find. Is there perhaps a slight sense of tingling, or warmth or no particular sensation?*
- *Next, allowing your awareness to move into the whole of the left leg.* (pause)
- *Now bring the focus of your awareness down the right leg, into the right foot, and bring that awareness down to your toes. What sensations do you notice there?*
- *Next, allowing your awareness to move into the whole of your right leg.* (pause)
- *See if you can move your focus, your awareness to the sensation in each arm and hand.* (pause)
- *Now focusing on your head and face, as best you can, bring a detailed level of awareness to the sensations present there.* (pause)

- *It is normal that your mind may wander away from a focus on the body. It is normal that you may start to feel bored with the activity. If you notice that, gently acknowledge it, noticing where the mind has gone off to, and start again, returning your attention to the part of the body you intended to focus on.*
- *Now move your focus to your chest and arms. As best you can, bring careful awareness to the sensations present in that area.* (pause)
- *Now, see if you can spend a few minutes being aware of the whole body, as well as the breath flowing in and out of the body.*

When you have finished, take a moment to record what you noticed, with colours and lines on a body outline.

SOMATIC FOCUS GROUNDING

Listening Inside

This mindfulness activity aims to help us make a direct connection with self, with our body and mood without our mind interrupting the experience. You may like to close your eyes to support an inward focus. Take a moment to get comfortable. Take a few slow full breaths.

See if you can become aware and focus on the movements of breath coming and going through the nose area and the chest. (pause)

See what you can notice, what you might be able to connect with. There is no right or wrong way to participate in this activity. The aim is not to try to change anything, but simply to keep an effort of attention alive.

Allow your awareness to continue to include the experience of breath coming and going, and expand from this to include awareness of physical sensations inside the whole body. Are there sensations you notice right now that you can use to ground your awareness inside?

See if you can become aware of a sense of the body as a whole and of any sensations in any parts of the body.

For example, can you become aware of the temperature of your body, or do you notice any tensions? You are not trying to change anything here, just to anchor your awareness inside yourself. See if you can become aware of physical sensations that arise where the body makes contact with the floor, chair, cushion or stool. See if you can become aware of physical sensations that arise from touch, pressure or contact of your feet with the floor. See if you can become aware of physical sensations that arise in your hands, where they rest on your body, or on each other.

As best you can, with awareness of these sensations, include the breath with the sense of the body as a whole. Be open to see if there is a particular mood at the moment. (pause)

If your body or your mood could speak, if they could inform you, what might they say right now? See if you can stay open and listen inside. Is there any response, it could be faint, it could be quiet. There may simply be an open space for a moment. See what your experience is.

Take your time. When you are ready, slowly bring your focus back into the room. You may like to let your body move or stretch. Take some time to quickly draw a body outline as large as you can on the page. Could you use colours and lines to show on the outline what you became aware of inside?

Write down any message or guidance that seemed to come from your body.

SELF-KINDNESS PRACTICE

May I Learn to Accept Myself

The reflection we are going to explore here will help you to remember to be kinder to yourself. It is ideal to use for yourself, especially at times when your inner critic seems more active and convincing.

Take a moment to feel where you are sitting, to feel where your body connects with the chair and to notice your breath is flowing by itself. Now, see if you could bring to mind a situation or an event in your life that caused you stress, or has activated your inner critic. While it is likely to be unpleasant to do this, there is a purpose here, to practice something we all need: self-kindness. See if you can actually feel or remember the stress or discomfort of this situation.

The next step is to recognise that the situation, or a moment of the event, or the commentary from your inner critic, did cause you some discomfort or a level of suffering.

See if you could stay with that moment the best you can, without trying to change or judge it. This effort to stay within inner experience is the practice of mindfulness. See if you could acknowledge the stress and any hurt feelings that arose.

Take another deep breath, and tune in again to your body and breath. Here we take a moment to acknowledge that our experience is not uncommon for people, that the discomfort, the suffering, is actually part of life. It is part of what humans share in. And we are part of humanity.

Take a moment to acknowledge that other people feel this way; we are not alone. All people struggle in life at times.

Take another deep breath, re-focus your attention on your body and mood. Now, slowly bring your hands over your heart area. Can you feel the warmth of your hands and the gentle touch of your hands on your chest? Or is there a different soothing touch that might feel right for you just now? Give your body a moment to experience the contact.

The next step in this activity is to deliberately send kindness to yourself. What would you need right now to hear that would convey kindness to yourself? Is there a phrase that speaks to you in your particular situation? You might like to listen and perhaps try out some of these, or they could inspire something new for you:

- *May I give myself the compassion that I need.*
- *May I learn to accept myself as I am.*
- *May I forgive myself.*
- *May I be strong.*
- *May I be patient.*

Sit with the feeling of this kindness for a moment. There is no hurry.

Might there be something from nature that could act as a reminder of this self-kindness? See if anything comes to mind. See if you would like to draw it, or express how you feel now with colours and lines on paper. Perhaps you would like to write something that will be a reminder.

PROGRESSIVE RELAXATION

Tension and Surrender

Find a comfortable position either sitting or, even better, lying down on a soft carpet or a yoga mat. Allow your attention to focus on your body. In this activity, we are going to bring attention and care to various areas of the body, hoping to bring connection and permission to relax. If you begin to notice your mind wandering, which is quite normal, bring your focus back to the muscle area you are working on.

Take a deep breath, down to your abdomen, hold for a few seconds and exhale slowly. Again, as you breathe, notice your stomach rising and your lungs filling with air.

Now let's begin (repeat each direction slowly, twice)*: Tune into your head. See if you can tighten the muscles in your forehead by raising your eyebrows as high as you can. Hold for a few seconds. And release.*

Let your mouth form a wide smile, feeling some tension in your mouth and cheeks. Hold for a moment, and release. After each action, take a moment to keep your awareness in the area you have tightened. Is it possible to connect with that part of your body? (Pause).

Next, tighten your eye muscles, and let your eyes close tightly shut. Hold for a moment, and release. (pause).

Gently tilt your head back as if to look at the ceiling. Hold for a moment, feel the tension and then release. See if you can imagine the tension melting away as you let go of the muscles. Breathe in…and out. In…and out. Let go as much as you can.

See if you can clench your fists and hold this position for a moment. And then release. Keep your awareness in the area you have tightened. Is it possible to connect with that part of your body? (pause)

Can you bring awareness to your arms? Flex the muscles of your upper arm. Hold for a moment, and release. Breathe in…and out. (pause)

Now raise your shoulders up as if they could touch your ears. Hold for a moment, and quickly release, let them be heavy. Repeat this. (pause)

Tense your upper back by pulling your shoulders back as if you were trying to make your shoulder blades touch. Hold for a moment, and release. (pause)

Bring awareness to your chest. See if you can tighten your chest by taking a deep breath in, hold for about 5 seconds and exhale, releasing as much of the tension as you can.

Now see if you can tighten the muscles in your stomach by pulling in lots of air. Hold for a moment, and release. Feel what that is like inside, then try it again. (pause)

Can you now move your awareness to your legs? Tune in there for a moment. Could you tighten your leg muscles, all the way from your feet up to your hips? Hold the tension for a moment, then surrender. (pause)

Now focus on your feet. Pull your toes towards you and feel which muscles are involved in this. Hold for a moment, and then relax. Imagine the weight of your legs sinking down into the carpet or floor. (pause)

Curl your toes under tensing your feet. Hold for about 5 seconds, release. (pause)

See if you can imagine a wave of relaxation slowly spreading through your body, beginning at your head and going all the way down to your feet.

Feel the weight of your body. Follow your breathing: in and out.

Can you take a moment to focus on your whole body, and watch and listen inside? What do you feel? Are there some colours, shapes or images that might go with what you are aware of?

Could you show this now with paper and crayons?

MINDFULNESS PRACTICE

Here and Now – In This Moment

This mindfulness activity combines short periods of focusing inside yourself, with expressing what you notice. This provides a gradual way to extend mindfulness moments over time, and it might be an activity you would like to repeat. The aim is to develop a practice for bringing yourself into the moment and being able to share about your effort.

There are four steps in this activity: taking time to focus on your thoughts, then on your breath as it flows in and out, then taking a moment to notice how your body feels, then seeing if you are aware of any mood or feelings.

The main elements of this mindfulness practice are to focus on not judging yourself or your efforts, practising and self-acceptance when you notice you are distracted, not trying to change or improve anything, and simply noticing – and staying with – what is happening in the present moment.

Step One – Noticing thoughts:

Find a way to sit that is comfortable, give your body permission to relax, and take a few slow full breaths and relax the breath out. See if it is possible to notice the thoughts in your mind. Can you recognise any comments, ideas or discussions with yourself going on? See if you can keep watching this for a moment. (pause)

When you are ready, write some notes, or use some colours and lines, to show something about the thoughts you noticed in your mind.

Step Two – Becoming aware of breath:

Come back to sitting comfortably, let your body relax again, and take a few slow full breaths and relax the breath out. For the next few minutes, see if you can simply experience your breathing. Don't change anything, simply feel the breath coming and going, and how your body moves as the breath flows. (pause)

When you are ready, stay in touch with the breath, and see if you could use some colours, lines or shapes to show how the breathing felt to you.

Step Three – Focusing inside the body:

Come back to sitting comfortably again, let your body relax, and take a few slow full breaths. This time, as you re-focus inside, bring your whole attention to your body. What is happening in there? Try to let go of thoughts about it, simply experience your muscles, your skin, your whole body. See if you can let your attention move around your body and connect with any tensions, sensations or pressures. What do you notice in your upper body? In your belly? In your legs? (pause)

When you are ready, see if you could use some colours and lines, shapes or pictures, in the body outline to show what you noticed.

Step Four – Emotional awareness:

Come back to sitting comfortably again, let your body relax, and take a few slow full breaths. This time, see if you can notice any moods or emotions, feelings or reactions. They could be in one place or spread out. There could be one mood, or more. It could be pleasant or uncomfortable. See what you notice. (pause)

When you are ready, see if you could use some colours and lines or shapes or pictures in the heart shape to show what you noticed.

Would you like to share anything about how you experienced the activity and what you found?

Was one of the four steps easier or more difficult?

Are there any times in your life when it might be useful to use this activity?

GROUNDING AND CENTRING

A Window to My Inner World

Let's stand up and run on the spot for a moment. You might like to give your body a shake.

Sit down in a way that is comfortable. Can you feel your heart beating after that run? This activity is an experiment to see how often you can let go of distractions and return your focus inside. Can you feel your breath coming and going? Can you feel yourself sitting in the chair? You may like to close your eyes to focus more clearly inside yourself.

Let your mind focus on feeling what is happening in your body now, and let your body become as soft and relaxed as possible. Could you let your neck relax a little? Could you let your shoulders drop, as you allow a fuller breath now? Check to make sure your abdomen is as relaxed as it can be, and let your legs and feet be soft now.

Let your breathing relax. Don't try to do anything with your breath.

Could you imagine you have a window to look inside yourself, not to see the muscles and bones and blood, but to feel where there might be some tensions or discomfort? Take a moment to allow a deeper focus inside.

You are simply watching your inner experience, not trying to do anything or change anything, whether it is pleasant or unpleasant. See if you can notice any thoughts or pictures in your mind, and let them pass by. See if it is possible for them to float away, as you keep watching inside.

Can you notice any feelings or moods? Take a moment with this. There is no right or wrong way to do this experiment. Let's see what you notice.

Can you notice sensations in your body. See if you can let go the urge to adjust or fix things. Simply be aware of all this. See if you can find a way to keep re-focusing inside.

Repeat

I will be quiet now. We can take some time to simply be aware inside, without a need to change anything. (long pause)

When you are ready, slowly and gently move your toes and fingers a little. Let your limbs stretch a bit, and when you are ready, let your eyes re-focus on the room.

Try to stay in touch with your inner experience as you look out at the outer world again.

Take some time to draw how you feel now, or write something about it.

You can express with any colours or shapes or pictures or words that came into your mind while we were sitting still.

We can talk about your experience soon.

MINDFUL MOVEMENT

Slow-Motion for Self-awareness

An aim of this activity is to work with focused attention, to connect with the body and the energy inside it. This activity can help the body loosen and relax, and it can also draw attention to tensions. There are lots of directions in this exercise and it may seem very controlled. If participants get in a muddle, acknowledge this, allow humour, relax, invite them to relax and take some full breaths and then continue. Soft, flowing background music may be very supportive.

Stand up and have a stretch. Take a deep breath. See if you can stand in a relaxed way with eyes closed.

Let your neck relax, allow your chin to move slowly down towards your chest. Do it very slowly, feel each degree of "let-go". It is as if you could be in the muscles. Take a moment for your whole body to explore letting go as your breath flows out.

Let your neck move slowly all the way down and then up so it is tilting back. See how slowly you can do this.

Bring your awareness now to your arms. Slowly raise your arms up in front of you until they are about level with your shoulders, then slowly let go. Let your wrists loose. Feel the use of tension as your arms rise, and then the degrees of letting go as they sink down again.

Bring your focus to your legs. Slowly bend your knees. Keep some awareness in the centre of you. See if you can feel the "let go" as the body goes down, and then the adding on of strength as you rise up. Keep the rest of the body more or less straight but not rigid.

See if it is possible to let your arms and knees move together now. The arms rise as the knees bend down. Each time you come up, feel the tall point. Keep allowing breath to release. Keep it all very slow.

See if you can let arms, wrists and knees flow together. There is no right or wrong way to do this. We are aiming to experience the body in movement from the inside. You cannot make a mistake here; it is all an experiment. If you get confused, simply begin again with just the arms, then add more. (pause)

Come to stillness now, and lie down. Take a moment to feel what it is like inside you. Is there a way you could express that? With art? With writing? With talking?

VISUALISATION AND ROLE-PLAY

I Am Nature

For this visualisation, I will invite you to welcome some pictures into your mind that go with the story I tell. Get comfortable, relax as much as you can, take a deep breath and tune into your body.

See if you can recall an area in nature which attracts you. This could be a place you love to be, a place that evokes awe, where you feel safe, happy, more in touch with yourself and more connected to the world. It could be a favourite beach, in the mountains, by a creek, it could be a lake, a river or a desert. It may include the sky, trees, flowers and beautiful views. It could be a special part of your own garden at home or a well-loved park.

Could you close your eyes for a moment, take a few deep breaths, and imagine being there now? What would you hear? Smell? What would you touch? What are the main things you would see?

Imagine moving through this place, or perhaps being still. Become interested in the details of what you remember. Take time and allow the images to soak in – enjoy them. (pause)

Now see if anything stands out for you? What is most noticeable? And see if you can feel the mood that goes with being in this place in nature.

When you are ready, you could do a quick sketch of the scene or the main images you remember.

Could you share a bit about the times you have been there? Do you remember anyone who was there with you? Could you say how you feel now after remembering this place, and how it made you feel to be there?

This next question may seem strange, but is there any way this beautiful place in nature is like you? Could you take a moment to imagine you are this beautiful place in nature? How does that feel?

If this place could speak, if it could give you any advice or encouragement, what might it say?

Could you write that down, perhaps on the drawing of the place? Would you like to add to your drawing – any further words or colours or lines?

SITTING PRACTICE

What Can I Hear Around Me?

See if you could practice mindful focus on your breath and body for a few minutes. Simply experience breath coming and going, and notice any sensations in your body. The aim is to return to breath awareness and body awareness. Let thoughts go as much as possible.

Allow your awareness to expand from your breath and body to hearing the sounds around you. Bring your attention to your ears. Let your awareness open and expand, so that you can welcome any sounds as they arise, sounds nearby, sounds in the distance.

As best you can, simply open your mind to receive sounds. Be aware of obvious sounds and of more subtle sounds, aware of the spaces between sounds, aware of any silence.

As best you can, be aware of sounds directly, without discussion about them in your head. When you find that you are thinking about the sounds, take a deep breath and reconnect to the task of listening. As best you can, come back to direct awareness of sounds, rather than thinking about or naming them.

If you notice that your awareness is no longer focused on sounds, gently acknowledge where your mind has wandered to, and reconnect with your breathing and body awareness. Then return your focus back to sounds.

If you notice thoughts filling your mind, acknowledge them without getting involved, then return focus to the sounds around you, no matter how quiet, faint or indistinct.

This mindfulness practice involves gently and consistently returning focus to sounds. See if you can remain open to the sounds, and include the movement of breathing and the sensations of your body again. I will be quite, see if you can continue to practice this mindful listening for a few minutes. (long pause)

Take a moment now to bring your focus to your internal state. How do you feel inside now?

When you are ready, slowly expand your awareness to include the room again, without abandoning your internal awareness. See if your body would like to move a little.

Could you write a few words or phrases that go with your internal experience?

Or, you might like to express your listening experience with colours and lines, or pictures.

VISUALISATION FOR PERSONAL GROWTH

No Stone Unturned

This is a visualisation activity to explore your personal growth over the last year, and to see if there is anything else you are called to focus on.

Could you lie back and relax, close your eyes and take a few deep breaths and relax them out?

Could you imagine you are out in nature, walking beside a river, up near its source? You are walking over and around pebbles, rocks and boulders. These are along the edge of the river as well as in it. The water is gently flowing over the pebbles and around the boulders.

Along the bank are many stones: smooth ones, rough ones, coloured ones. Under some of these stones lie pictures of the areas of personal growth you have explored over the last year.

Could you imagine yourself now stepping forward, going upstream along the bank? You come to an interesting stone now. Bend down and turn it over. See the picture underneath it, it is a picture of something you have learned about your life, about yourself or some way you have grown. What do you see? (pause)

After looking at the picture for a moment, see if you could quickly sketch the stone on the art paper and the picture you saw on it. You might also like to jot down any words that go with this aspect of your growth. (pause)

When you are ready, take another deep breath, settle back and picture yourself continuing this walk beside the river. You are watching the stones.

See if there is another that attracts your attention. Bend down and turn it over. See the picture underneath it, it is a picture of something you have learned about your life, about yourself, or some way you have grown. What do you see? (pause)

After looking at the picture for a moment, see if you could sketch the stone and the picture you saw on the stone. You might also like to jot down any words that go with this part of your growth. (pause)

When you are ready, take another deep breath, settle back and picture yourself continuing this walk beside the river. You are watching the stones.

Now you come to an odd-shaped stone that is an unusual colour. You are drawn to it. You lift it up, turn it over. Underneath it, you find a picture of something in your personal growth that is ahead of you. This stone may be showing you something about your future growth. Look carefully, let it reveal its picture.

After looking at the picture for a moment, see if you could sketch the stone and the picture you saw. You might also like to jot down any words that go with this part of your growth. (pause)

When you are ready, see what you would like to share about the pictures on the stones, anything you drew or wrote about.

MINDFUL ENERGY FOCUS

Finding My Neutral Observer

This activity can help wake up our energy in a way that helps us connect with ourselves more fully.

Let's stand up and stretch. Give your body a shake. Take a few deep, full breaths.

Let's create some rhythms with clapping and movement. It may feel odd, but moving, clapping and finding a rhythm can help us wake up and feel more alive. Let's see if we can go faster and faster for a moment. Let's speed up the rhythm!

Now: total body surrender. Let your body flop down, relax, melt down onto the floor. Let's see if it is possible to establish a place inside that is aiming to be a neutral observer, that can watch "just what is".

It's time to surrender to observing the sensations and energy in your body without comment. See if you can come into a closer relationship with yourself.

I will invite you to turn on your neutral observer to explore body reading from the inside. Let's do this now: focus on your head and face for a moment. How does it feel in there?

Allow your neutral observer to focus on your chest. Take some time to receive the experience of that area. (pause) I will be quiet now, while you focus into your arms and hands, then your abdomen, then finally your legs and feet. Take your time, there is no hurry. (long pause)

Surrender again, lying on the floor, soften, open, melt. Bring your hands to create a soft touch on your chest or abdomen. Notice how this feels from the inside.

Take a moment to ponder how you would most want to care for yourself. With compassion for yourself, what do you wish for yourself? Take a moment to simply be with that question. (pause)

When you feel ready, see if you would like to write or draw, to capture your awareness and your wish for self-care.

VISUALISATION

A Glimpse of My Potential

Let yourself rest, maybe lie on a carpeted floor or yoga mat. Turn your focus inside. Relax as much as possible, let your body soften. You may find it helps your inner focus to let your eyes close. Take a few moments to gently hum. See if you can focus humming in your upper body, and then in your lower body.

Bring your hands to rest over your heart area, and bring your internal focus there, see if you can feel your heart space from the inside.

In this visualisation, allow images to appear in your mind that go with the words you hear spoken. It may take a moment. Wait for them to come. See the images as clearly as you can in your mind, see colours, watch for details. As we proceed, see if you can stay connected to your heart space. If no images appear. Simply allow yourself to continue to breathe and bring a softening to your body.

Can you include with your internal focus, the feeling, perhaps a longing, for a time of deeper healing, a time when you feel your personal growth has developed and you find yourself more often in a positive state? See if you can picture a time like this in the not-too-distant future. Take a moment to watch inside for any responses to this suggestion.

Images of this future time can help you be in touch with your future potential; a time when you feel you are past old worries and disappointments.

Let yourself imagine a time when you are free from early conditioning and can enjoy a greater sense of freedom and spontaneity in your choices. This might be a time when you feel you know yourself more fully, and there are few fears about your inner world. See if you can picture this as a time when you are more often guided by what would be your Essential Self.

Where would you be? Could you picture the environment where you might live? What work would you be doing?

What activities would you be engaged with, what activities might you feel "called" to do? What interests might you seek to follow?

Are there people with you? Who is nearby? Perhaps you can picture specific people or people in general.

Take some deep breaths, and see if you can stay with this glimpse of your personal growth potential.

When you feel ready, bring your focus slowly and easefully back to the outside world. Consider if you would like to draw or write about the images that were presented from within.

See if you would like to record any steps you could make, or would want to make, in your life now, towards this potential.

RELAXATION AND GUIDED MEDITATION

Can I Find a Quiet Centre?

This will be a quiet sitting meditation. But first, stand up and stretch. Take a few deep breaths. Could you take a moment to shake off any stresses of the day? Try running on the spot for a moment as you shake. (pause)

Now, slow down and stop. Take a moment to tune into your breathing and heart rate. Let your body calm down.

Sit down in a position that is comfortable and relaxing. Close your eyes and take a moment to feel your breath coming and going. Can you feel any result inside after that running? Just be with that for a moment. (pause)

Let your body be as soft and relaxed as possible. Let your attention focus on what is happening in your body now.

See if it is possible to allow a deeper letting go in your body. Could you let your neck relax and go a little bit softer at the back? Tune into your shoulders and let them drop. See if your belly could relax a little more. Feel your feet resting on the floor, and let your legs and feet be soft.

Let your breathing relax. Don't try to do anything with your breath. Let it do its work without any effort from you.

You are simply watching inside now. What are the main sensations in your body? (pause)

What are the main thoughts or pictures in your mind? Can you find a place inside from which to observe thoughts or images that float by? (pause)

Without changing anything, see if you notice a mood or emotion inside. Is it possible to notice what you are feeling right now? (pause)

Simply be aware of all this. You might like to choose a single focus for your attention for the next stage, or you may like to gently scan between observing thoughts, feelings and sensations.

I will be quiet now. We can take some time to simply be aware inside. (longer pause)

When you are ready, slowly and gently move your toes and fingers a little. Let your limbs stretch a bit, and when you are ready, let your eyes open. Try to stay in touch with your inner world as you look out at the outer world again.

Take some time to draw a circle, and then use any colours, shapes or pictures in or around the circle to express any responses to the activity, and responses to what you observed while you were sitting still. We can talk about the activity soon.

Would you like to share anything about how you found the meditation?

Would you like to say anything about any difficulties in focusing your attention, and what most helps?

Do you have any ideas about when it might be most useful to work with this activity?

EXPRESSING REFLECTIONS

Finding Myself in Nature

This activity is about reflecting back on a recent peaceful time in nature that you enjoyed, and expressing – in art form and writing – the sensations, feelings and impressions of that day.

On the art paper, draw a large circle that will be used as a place to express your feelings about the time in nature that this activity invites you to reflect on.

You might like to sit comfortably or perhaps lie back on a carpeted floor or yoga mat for this reflection activity.

Take a few moments now to connect with yourself, with your breathing. Relax as much as you can, and see what it would mean for you to "tune in", to "come home" to yourself. (pause)

In the past few days, have there been any aspects of nature you have particularly noticed? For example, the wind, rain, temperature, sun, trees, grasses, flowers, water and the changing light?

What has been your relationship with nature, with places in nature, over recent days or weeks? Simply allow any memories or pictures to form in your mind. (pause)

Take a moment now to see if you can recall a recent day when you spent some peaceful time in nature that you enjoyed. See what memory comes to mind. (pause)

See if you can relax and let the memory come to you. Start to recall a place, a time, when you were in a natural setting. See if you can recall what you looked at, what you heard and what you could smell. Take a breath, and allow yourself to see clearly, to recall that time in nature that you enjoyed.

Can you also recall anything about how you felt inside at that time? Did you notice any mood or emotions that day? (longer pause)

Take a moment to notice how you feel inside right now. Check in with your body, mood and thoughts. What do you notice right now?

When you feel ready, you might like to use colour, line, images and words to express something from your experiences during this activity.

ENERGY CENTRE MEDITATION

Heart and Belly Focus

Find a comfortable way to sit. Allow your body to relax as much as it can. Take a few deep breaths.

Move your attention to your chest. Tune in there for a moment. Can you feel it rise and fall?

(pause)

Now see if you can move your attention down to your belly. See if you can feel it from the inside, let it relax and hang loose. (pause)

As you breathe in, move your attention to your chest for a while. (pause). *On the next out-breath, be aware of dropping your awareness down to focus on your belly.* (repeat).

Your attention will simply fall and rise between the heart area and the belly area, along with the breathing.

Let your breathing remain natural and relaxed. Even if you get distracted, come back to moving the focus of awareness with each breath.

We will work this way for a while, feeling first the chest from the inside, then the belly.

There is nothing else to do. See if you can simply stay focused inside yourself.

Every time a new thought comes into your mind, and you realise it has taken your attention away from the exercise, sigh out all your breath as if you were sighing out the thoughts that get in the way.

Then begin again. In this exercise, it is normal to begin again and again.

Support the client to work this way for a few minutes.

Appendix

Suggested Background Music for Relaxation, Meditation and Visualisation

• *Inner Peace / Relaxation Suite*	Steven Halpern
• *Music for Yoga*	Steven Halpern + much more
• *Mariner / Wind Seeker / Complete Calm*	Tony O'Connor + much more
• *Moonstone*	Stairway - especially tracks 4, 5 and 9
• *Pan Flutes by the Ocean*	Ken Davis + much more
• *Initiation / Stillpoint*	Gabrielle Roth + much more
• *The Secret Garden*	David Sun (long tracks 20mins!)
• *Tranquillity*	David Sun (long tracks 20mins!)
• *Songs from a Secret Garden*	Secret Garden
• *Music to Disappear In Vol 2*	Raphael + much more
• *Tantra – Spiritual Environment*	Anugama (long tracks 25mins!)
• *Healing – Relaxation Environment*	Anugama (long tracks 25mins)+ lots more
• *Chakra Dance*	Malcolm Stern / Stairway especially tracks 7 and 8
• *Music for Relaxation*	Chapman, Miles, Rhodes (New World)
• *Yoga Harmony*	Terry Oldfield + lots more
• *Reiki*	Llewellyn
• *Reiki – Hands of Light*	Deuter (long tracks 10mins +)
• *Keeper of Dreams / Heavenly Realms*	Philip Chapman
• *Music for Yoga*	Various Artists
• *Crystal Cascades*	Christopher Buckman

References

Babouchkina, A., & Robbins, S. J. (2015). Reducing negative mood through mandala creation: A randomized controlled trial. *Art Therapy, 32*(1), 34–39. https://doi.org/10.1080/07421656.2015.994428

Barragan-Jason, G., Loreau, M., de Mazancourt, C., Singer, M. C., & Parmesan, C. (2023). Psychological and physical connections with nature improve both human well-being and nature conservation: A systematic review of meta-analyses. *Biological Conservation, 277*, 109842. https://doi.org/10.1016/j.biocon.2022.109842

Baylis, P. J., Collins, D., & Coleman, H. (2011). Child alliance process theory: A qualitative study of a child centred therapeutic alliance. *Child and Adolescent Social Work Journal, 28*(2), 79–95.

Benson, H., & Klipper, M. Z. (2000). *The relaxation response.* Harper Collins.

Cain, M. (2019). "But It Wouldn't Be Me": Exploring empathy and compassion for self and others through creative processes. In G. Barton & S. Garvis (eds.), *Compassion and empathy in educational contexts* (pp. 39–57). Palgrave Macmillan.

Cain, M. (2023). 'Those moments are ineffable'. How creativity experienced through the arts promotes empathy and compassion. *Journal of Moral Education, 54*(3), 438–454. https://doi.org/10.1080/03057240.2023.2287397

Carey, L. J. (2006). *Expressive and creative arts methods for trauma survivors.* Jessica Kingsley Publishers.

Carletto, S., Borghi, M., Bertino, G., Oliva, F., Cavallo, M., Hofmann, A., ... & Ostacoli, L. (2016). Treating post-traumatic stress disorder in patients with multiple sclerosis: A randomized controlled trial comparing the efficacy of eye movement desensitization and reprocessing and relaxation therapy. *Frontiers in Psychology, 7*, 526.

Carlson, C. R., & Hoyle, R. H. (1993). Efficacy of abbreviated progressive muscle relaxation training: A Quantitative review of behavioural medicine research. *Journal of Consulting and Clinical Psychology, 61*(6), 1059–1067.

Corey, G. (2008). *Theory and practice of group counselling.* Brooks / Cole.

Csikszentmihalyi, M. (1997). *Creativity: Flow and the psychology of discovery and invention.* HarperCollins Publishers.

Curry, N. A., & Kasser, T. (2005). Can coloring mandalas reduce anxiety? *Art Therapy, 22*(2), 81–85.

Dance, C. J., Ipser, A., & Simner, J. (2022). The prevalence of aphantasia (imagery weakness) in the general population. *Consciousness and Cognition, 97*, 103243.

Davidson, R. J., Kabat-Zinn, J., Schumacher, J., Rosenkranz, M., Muller, D., Santorelli, S. F., ... & Sheridan, J. F. (2003). Alterations in brain and immune function produced by mindfulness meditation. *Psychosomatic Medicine, 65*(4), 564–570.

DeLucia-Waack, J. L. (2006). *Leading psychoeducational groups for children and adolescents*. Sage Publications.

Felder, J. N., Dimidjian, S., & Segal, Z. (2012). Collaboration in mindfulness-based cognitive therapy. *Journal of Clinical Psychology, 68*(2), 179–186.

Field, T. A. (2014). Integrating left-brain and right-brain: The neuroscience of effective counseling. *The Professional Counselor, 4*(1), 19–27.

Fredrickson, B. L. (2001). The role of positive emotions in positive psychology: The broaden-and-build theory of positive emotions. *American Psychologist, 56*(3), 218–226.

Geller, S. M., & Greenberg, L. S. (2012). *Therapeutic presence: A mindful approach to effective therapy*. American Psychological Association.

Germer, C. K. (2005). Mindfulness: What is it? What does it matter? In C. K. Germer, R. D. Siegel, & P. R. Fulton (Eds.), *Mindfulness and psychotherapy* (pp. 3–27). Guilford Press.

Germer, C. K. (2009). *The mindful path to self-compassion: Freeing yourself from destructive thoughts and emotions*. The Guilford Press.

Gilbert, P. (2009). *The compassionate mind*. Constable and Robinson.

Gilbert, P., & Irons, C. (2004). A pilot exploration of the use of compassionate images in a group of self-critical people. *Memory, 12*, 507–516.

Gilbert, P., Baldwin, M. W., Irons, C., Baccus, J. R., & Palmer, M. (2006). Self-criticism and self-warmth: An imagery study exploring their relation to depression. *Journal of Cognitive Psychotherapy, 20*(2), 183–200.

Gilbert, P., Clarke, M., Hempel, S., Miles, J. N. V., & Irons, C. (2004). Criticizing and reassuring one-self: An exploration of forms, styles and reasons in female students. *British Journal of Clinical Psychology, 43*, 31–50. https://doi.org/10.1348/014466504772812959

Gilbert, P., McEwan, K., Matos, M., & Rivis, A. (2011). Fears of compassion: Development of three self-report measures. *Psychology and Psychotherapy: Theory, Research and Practice, 84*(3), 239–255.

Goldfried, M. R., & Trier, C. S. (1974). Effectiveness of relaxation as an active coping skill. *Journal of Abnormal Psychology, 83*(4), 348–355.

Goodman, T. A. (2013). Working with children. Beginner's mind. In C. K. Germer, R. D. Siegel, & P. R. Fulton (Eds.), *Mindfulness and psychotherapy* (pp. 239–258). The Guilford Press.

Grepmair, L., Mitterlehner, F., Loew, T., Bachler, E., Rother, W., & Nickel, M. (2007). Promoting mindfulness in psychotherapists in training influences the treatment results of their patients: A randomized, double-blind, controlled study. *Psychotherapy and Psychosomatics, 76*(6), 332–338. https://doi.org/10.1159/000107560

Grof, S., Grof, C., & Kornfield, J. (2010). *Holotropic breathwork: A new approach to self-exploration and therapy*. SUNY Press.

Hinterkopf, E. (1998). *Integrating spirituality in counseling: A manual for using the experiential focusing method*. American Counseling Association.

Holian, L. (2001). *Metacognition: Highlighting the importance of emotional reflection and expression*. Unpublished master's project, Monash University, Victoria, Australia.

Holmes, E. A., & Matthews, A. (2010). Mental imagery in emotion and emotional disorders. *Clinical Psychology Review, 30*(3), 349–362.

Holmes, E. A., Mathews, A., Mackintosh, B., & Dalgleish, T. (2008). The causal effect of mental imagery on emotion assessed using picture-word cues. *Emotion, 8*(3), 395–409.

Holm-Hadulla, R. M., & Hofmann, F. (2012). Counselling, psychotherapy and creativity. *Asia Pacific Journal of Counselling and Psychotherapy, 3*(2), 130–136.

Hoult, L. M., Wetherell, M. A., Edginton, T., & Smith, M. A. (2025). Positive expressive writing interventions, subjective health and wellbeing in non-clinical populations: A systematic review. *PLoS One, 20*(5), e0308928.

Hycner, R., & Jacobs, L. (1995). *The healing relationship in Gestalt Therapy: A dialogical/self psychology approach.* Gestalt Journal Press.

Jacobs, J. B. (1990). Extended mutual imagery in work with anxious and phobic clients. *Clinical Social Work Journal, 18*(2), 175–185.

Jones, C., & Gwenin, C. (2021). Cortisol level dysregulation and its prevalence. Is it nature's alarm clock? *Physiological Reports, 8*(24), e14644.

Jones, V. L., Salgado García, F. I., Brewer, L. M., Pérez-Muñoz, A., Schenck, L. A. M., You, Z., & Andrasik, F. (2023). The relaxation zone: Initial analysis of stress management services for university students. *Journal of American College Health, 71*(7), 2106–2114.

Jung, C. G. (1973). *Mandala symbolism.* Bollingen Series.

Kabat-Zinn, J. (1994). *Wherever you go, there you are.* Hyperion.

Kabat-Zinn, J. (2013). *Full catastrophe living, revised edition: How to cope with stress, pain and illness using mindfulness meditation.* Hachette UK.

Karris, M., & Caldwell, B. E. (2015). Integrating Emotionally Focused Therapy, self-compassion, and Compassion-Focused Therapy to assist shame-prone couples who have experienced trauma. *The Family Journal: Counseling and Therapy for Couples and Families, 23*(4), 346–357.

Kellogg, J. (1992). Color therapy from the perspective of the great round of mandala. *Journal of Religion and Psychical Research, 15*(2), 138–146.

Kenardy, J., & Piercy, J., A. (2006). Effect of information provision on trauma symptoms following therapeutic writing. *Australian Psychologist, 41*(3), 205–218.

Kima, H., Kima, S., Choeb, K., & Kimb, J. (2018). Effects of mandala art therapy on subjective well-being, resilience, and hope in psychiatric inpatients. *Archives of Psychiatric Nursing, 32*, 167–173. https://dx. doi.org/10.1016/j.apnu.2017.08.008

Knagg, H., Pratt, D., Taylor, P. J., & Palmier-Claus, J. (2021). A positive mental imagery intervention for targeting suicidal ideation in university students: A pilot study. *Clinical Psychology and Psychotherapy, 29*(4), 1392–1402.

Li, B., Zhu, Q., Li, A., & Cui, R. (2023). Can good memories of the past instill happiness? Nostalgia improves subjective well-being by increasing gratitude. *Journal of Happiness Studies, 24*(2), 699–715.

Lovas, J. (2015). Evidence-based relaxation therapy: physiological and psychological benefits. *Journal of the Australian Traditional-Medicine Society, 21*(2), 105.

Lusebrink, V. B. (1990). *Imagery and visual expression in therapy.* Plenum Press.

Malchiodi, C, (2020). *Trauma and expressive arts therapy. Brain, body, and imagination in the healing process.* The Guilford Press.

Mandel, S. E., Davis, B. A., & Secic, M. (2013). Effects of music therapy and music-assisted relaxation and imagery on health-related outcomes in diabetes education: A feasibility study. *The Diabetes Educator, 39*(4), 568–581.

Maslow, A. H. (1962). Some basic propositions of a growth and self-actualization psychology. In A. W. Coombs (Ed.), *Perceiving, behaving, becoming: A new focus for education* (pp. 34–49). National Education Association.

McMurray, M., & Schwartz-Mirman, O. (2001). Integration and working through in art therapy. *The Arts in Psychotherapy, 28*(5), 311–318.

Morton, K., & Cescato, M. (2000). The efficacy of relaxation training with Year 12 students. *Australian Journal of Guidance* and *Counselling, 10*(1), 133–144.

Muran, J. C., & Barber, J. P. (2010). *The therapeutic alliance. An evidence-based guide to practice*. The Guilford Press.

Nathan, L. F. (2019). Creativity, the arts, and the future of work. In J. W. Cook (Ed.), *Sustainability, human well-being, and the future of education* (pp. 283–310). Palgrave MacMillan.

Neff, K. D. (2003). Self-compassion: An alternative conceptualization of a healthy attitude toward oneself. *Self and Identity, 2*(2), 85–101. https://doi.org/10.1080/15298860309032

Neff, K. D., Kirkpatrick, K. L., & Rude, S. S. (2007). Self-compassion and adaptive psychological functioning. *Journal of Research in Personality, 41*(1), 139–154. https://doi.org/10.1016/j.jrp.2006.03.004

Neff, K. D., & Vonk, R. (2009). Self-compassion versus global self-esteem: Two different ways of relating to oneself. *Journal of Personality, 77*(1), 23–50. https://doi.org/10.1111/j.1467-6494.2008.00537.x

Nurlela, N., & Jannati, Z. (2019). Relaxation technique within group counseling to reduce student's anxiety on facing exam. *Islamic Guidance and Counseling Journal, 2*(1), 33–39.

Ost, L. G. (1987). Applied relaxation: Description of a coping technique and review of controlled studies. *Behaviour Research and Therapy, 25*(5), 397–409.

Pearson, M. (2019). Counselling intern self-awareness and readiness for practice: Reports from a mindfulness challenge. *Asia-Pacific Journal of Counselling & Psychotherapy*, 11(1), 23–33. https://doi.org/10.1080/21507686.2019.1703772

Pearson, M., & Wilson, H. (2009). *Using expressive arts to work with mind, body and emotions. Theory and practice.* Jessica Kingsley Publishers.

Pearson, M., & Wilson, H. (2024). Guiding clients towards self-kindness and acceptance: Wrestling with the inner critic. *Psychotherapy and Counselling Journal of Australia.* https://pacja.org.au/article/123356-guiding-clients-towards-self-kindness-and-acceptance-wrestling-with-the-inner-critic

Peiris, C. L., O'Donoghue, G., Rippon, L., Meyers, D., Hahne, A., De Noronha, M., ... & Hanson, L. C. (2021). Classroom movement breaks reduce sedentary behavior and increase concentration, alertness and enjoyment during university classes: A mixed-methods feasibility study. *International Journal of Environmental Research and Public Health, 18*(11), 5589.

Pennebaker, J. W., & Seagal, J. D. (1999). Forming a story: The health benefits of narrative. *Journal of Clinical Psychology, 55*, 1243–1254.

Perry, B. D. (2006). Applying principles of neurodevelopment to clinical work with maltreated and traumatized children: The neurosequential model of therapeutics. In N. B. Webb (Ed.), *Working with traumatized youth in child welfare* (pp. 27–52). The Guilford Press.

Peterkin, A. D., & Prettyman, A. A. (2009). Finding a voice: Revisiting the history of therapeutic writing. *Medical Humanities, 35*(2), 80–88. https://doi.org/10.1136/jmh.2009.001636

Pisarik, C. T., & Larson, K. R. (2011). Facilitating college students' authenticity and psychological well-being through the use of mandalas: An empirical study. *Journal of Humanistic Counseling, 50*, 84–98.

Rogers, C. R. (2051). *Client-centered therapy: Its current practice, implications and theory*. Houghton Mifflin.

Rosenberg, M. S., Wilson, R., Maheady, L., & Sindelar, P. T. (1997). *Educating students with behavior disorders* (2nd edn). Allyn & Bacon.

Rothschild, B. (2010). *The body remembers. The psychophysiology of trauma and trauma treatment*. W. W. Norton & Company.

Ruini, C., & Mortara, C. C. (2022). Writing technique across psychotherapies - From traditional expressive writing to new positive psychology interventions: A narrative review. *Journal of Contemporary Psychotherapy, 52*, 23–34. https://doi.org/10.1007/s10879-021-09520-9

Russell, R., Guerry, A. D., Balvanera, P., Gould, R. K., Basurto, X., Chan, K. M., ... & Tam, J. (2013). Humans and nature: How knowing and experiencing nature affect well-being. *Annual Review of Environment and Resources, 38*(1), 473–502.

Segal, Z. V., Williams, J. M. G., & Teasdale, J. D. (2002). *Mindfulness-based cognitive therapy for depression: A new approach to preventing relapse*. The Guilford Press.

Seligman, M. E. (2002). Positive psychology, positive prevention, and positive therapy. In C. R. Snyder & S. J. Lopez (Eds.), *Handbook of positive psychology* (pp. 3–12). Oxford University Press.

Segal, Z., Williams, M., & Teasdale, J. (2012). *Mindfulness-based cognitive therapy for depression*. Guilford Press.

Siegel, D. (2007). *The mindful brain: Reflection and attunement in the cultivation of well-being*. W. W. Norton & Co.

Smitheman-Brown, V., & Church, R. P. (1996). Mandala drawing: Facilitating creative growth in children with A.D.D. or A.D.H.D. *Art Therapy: Journal of the American Art Therapy Association, 13*(4), 252–260.

Sosin, L. S., Noble, S. D., Harrichand, J. J. S., & Bohecker, L. (2022). The Creative Arts Personal Growth Group (CAPG): Transforming fear and shame. *The Journal for Specialists in Group Work, 47*(2), 151–167. https://doi.org/10.1080/01933922.2021.2000083

Strand, M., & Stige, S. H. (2021). Combining mindfulness and compassion in the treatment of complex trauma–A theoretical exploration. *European Journal of Trauma & Dissociation, 5*(3), 100217.

Van Der Vennet, R., & Serice, S. (2012). Can coloring mandalas reduce anxiety? A replication study. *Art Therapy, 29*(2), 87–92.

van Westrhenen, N., Fritz, E., Oosthuizen, H., Lemont, S., Vermeer, A., & Kleber, R. J. (2017). Creative arts in psychotherapy treatment protocol for children after trauma. *The Arts in Psychotherapy, 54*, 128–135.

Vasu, D. T., Nordin, N. A. M., Xu, S. X., Ghazali, S. E., & Zarim, S. N. A. (2020). Feasibility and outcomes of autogenic relaxation training in addition to usual physiotherapy for stroke survivors - a pilot study. *Malaysian Journal of Public Health Medicine, 20*(3), 134–139.

Victoria, H. K., & Caldwell, C. (2013). Breathwork in body psychotherapy: Clinical applications. *Body, Movement and Dance in Psychotherapy, 8*(4), 216–228.

Whitfield, H. J. (2006). Towards case-specific applications of mindfulness-based cognitive-behavioural therapies: A mindfulness-based rational emotive behaviour therapy. *Counselling Psychology Quarterly, 19*(2), 205–217.

Young, A. J. (2001). Mandalas - Circling the square in education. *Encounter: Education for Meaning and Social Justice, 14*(3), 25–33.

Index

agitation 8
autogenic phrases 19–20, 76

breath 8, 30, 45–46, 93

clay 24, 38
creativity 3, 12, 16

drawing 4, 6, 11, 24, 36

evidence base 21
expectations 9, 23–24
expressive writing 10, 37

gratitude 10, 19, 96
grounding 86, 101, 103, 109
group work 12–15
guided imagery 80

imagination 15
inner critic 9, 18, 104
invitational relating style 5, 9

Kabat-Zinn, J. 21, 99

mandalas 11, 24, 34, 35
meditation 8, 21, 82, 84, 87, 91, 93, 97, 116, 118
mental imagery *see* visualisation
mindfulness 3, 20–26, 99, 107
movement 9, 49, 61, 63–66, 82, 84, 110
music 7, 10, 11, 13, 17, 35, 119

nature 52, 71, 111, 117

peace 54, 60
positive psychology 18
progressive relaxation 19

rapport 6–7
relaxation 3, 19–20, 41, 50, 105

self-care 3, 19, 32
self-compassion 26–27, 31, 32, 104
self-criticism 18, 31
self-kindness *see* self-compassion
self-reflective writing 9–10
somatic awareness 40, 89, 91, 101, 103
symbols 15–17

tension 9, 22, 47, 105
therapeutic presence 4–5

visualisation 16–18, 47, 111, 113, 115